MILLENNIALS 2.0
Empowering Generation Y

By

Jan Ferri-Reed, Ph.D.

Published by:

KEYGroup Press
1800 Sainte Claire Plaza
1121 Boyce Road
Pittsburgh, PA 15241-3918
Phone: 724-942-7900
Toll Free: 1-800-456-5790

Requests for permission should be sent to:
KEYGroup Press
1800 Sainte Claire Plaza
1121 Boyce Road
Pittsburgh, PA 15241-3918
Toll Free: 1-800-456-5790
Phone: 724-942-7900

Printed in the United States of America .

ISBN: 978-0-9654465-9-4

CONTENTS

Chapter 1: The Promise of a "Lost Generation" 1

    Strategies for Building a Millennial-Friendly Workplace 8

    You May Be a Millennial If 9

Chapter 2: Recognizing a New Type of Employee 15

    Strategies for Onboarding Millennials 24

    You May Be a Gen Exer If 25

Chapter 3: Controlling Intergenerational Conflict 31

    Strategies for Managing Conflict 42

Chapter 4: The New Definition of Engagement 47

    Strategies for Mentoring Millennials 57

    You May Be a Baby Boomer If 58

Chapter 5: Motivating Millennials with Work-Flex 63

    Strategies for Implementing Work-Flex 71

Chapter 6: Cultivating the Leaders of the Future 77

    Strategies for Cultivating Millennial Leaders 82

    You May Be a Mature If 83

Chapter 7: Empowering Your Millennials 89

    Strategies for Empowering Millennials 100

Chapter 8: Millennials in the Real World 105

Preface

The world is the midst of a revolution that will ultimately transform everything. The Millennial generation is rising rapidly and taking their place alongside the generations that came before them. Generation Y is perhaps the best educated generation in history, but they bring with them unique perceptions and a differing work ethic that often confounds and antagonizes older generations, especially the Baby Boomers.

Our consulting organization, KEYGroup, first began receiving numerous requests back in the early 2000's for workshops and keynote speeches on how to deal with the next generation. Most of the time we heard "Who are these kids and just who do they think they are anyway?" After hearing this and other angst-ridden (and sometimes non-flattering) comments about Generation Y from clients, the late Dr. Joanne G. Sujansky and I added Generation Y programs to our core offering of services to help organizations recruit, develop and retain talent.

After extensive research we began offering programs about managing Generation Y, which led eventually to our first book on this subject, *Keeping the Millennials: Why Companies Are Losing Billions of Dollars to This Generation and What To Do About It*, which was published in 2009 by John Wiley & Sons, Inc. That book answered numerous needs and problems, but in the years following publication KEYGroup continued to be flooded with requests for strategies, techniques, job aids and resources to retain the talent of all generations.

But the Millennials, due to the impact of their astounding numbers and their major influence upon today's organizations, remain a vital, challenging and promising topic of concern throughout the workplace. And so, the logical next step was *Millennials 2.0: Empowering Generation Y*, a volume filled with best-practice strategies and practical techniques for managing the new generation.

And, as the parent of a Millennial I've watched as my son and the Millennial children of my colleagues take their places in today's workplace, with all of the enthusiasm, fresh thinking, and unique perspectives that are the legacy of every new generation.

The purpose of this book is to pick up where Keeping the Millennials left off. We understand better than ever why Millennials are the way they are and what they expect. We know that forward-thinking organizations and leaders continue to evolve their company cultures to attract more youth.

We also know that Millennials are here to stay and will soon become the dominant generation in every workplace. So now, more than ever, leaders are wise to ramp up their leadership strategies. By engaging their Millennial employees leaders will be able to merge their company's mission with the values, insights and aspirations of the incoming generation!

Acknowledgements

First and foremost, David G. Young has been a gem, once again managing the complete (and I might add painstakingly detailed) process of the manuscript research, editing and formatting. Thanks, Dave – for all you do. I would also like to thank Chuck Sujansky, KEYGroup CEO, for the support, funding and general oversight of the project. Kelly Parker Hanna has not only fueled the marketing and promotion of keynotes and writing but has also continued to prod me to stay on schedule – "Chop, chop!" as Kel would say. Thanks to Patti Dubbs and Taylor Thomas for all your help with the marketing. And, last but not least, Joanne…your vision, passion and unfailing support still lives in my heart. This book is dedicated to you and your legacy.

Jan Ferri-Reed, Ph.D.

For over 24 years, Jan Ferri-Reed, the president of KEY-Group, has worked with leaders to create cool workplaces that attract, retain, and get the most from their talent. Her expertise, insight, wisdom, humor, and practical solutions have made Jan a highly sought-after speaker for keynote addresses, seminars, conferences, and workshops. She has brought fresh concepts and effective techniques to executives and audiences around the globe. Client favorites include the following topics:

- Motivating and Retaining Talent: Keeping Your Keepers
- Keys to Creating the Productive, Profitable Workplaces
- Why Keep The Ys? The Keys To Creating Cool Workplaces
- Maintaining Resilience

Among the organizations that have engaged Jan to deliver speeches, develop custom presentations, and provide consulting services are: GlaxoSmithKline, Pitney Bowes, PPG Industries, Inc., U.S. Steel Corporation, SAE International, American Society of Association Executives, Transformer Association, The Minerals, Metals & Materials Society, National Association of Graphic and Product Identification Manufacturers, Inc., Bristol Myers Squibb, Bayer, Mitsubishi Electric Power Products, and MTV Networks. She is the co-author of the recently published book with Dr. Joanne G. Sujansky for John Wiley Publications, *Keeping the Millennials: Why Companies are Losing Billions in Turnover to This Generation and What to Do About It.* The book explains how Millennials are costing corporations around the globe billions in unnecessary, preventable turnover and provides a proven approach for creating a corporate culture that keeps them on the job and working productively.

Jan has been called upon by numerous media sources to provide guidance on leadership practices and productive workplace cultures. She is also an active member of the American Society for Training and Development (ASTD), the HR Leadership Forum, and Pittsburgh Human Resources Association (PHRA).

She has served on the Board of the Association for The Arc and on the Advisory Board of the Association for Children and Adults with Learning Disabilities. Her doctoral work was completed at the University of Pittsburgh where her studies focused in the areas of consultant ethics and organizational development. Additionally, Jan was an adjunct professor to the Human Resources Management Program at LaRoche University.

Her energy and sense of purpose translate into winning presentations that audiences applaud. Packed with plenty of take-home value and on-the-job applicability, you can count on Jan's presentations to provide you with the keys to unlock the leader within you, your team, and your organization.

The young do not know enough to be prudent,
and therefore they attempt the impossible
-- and achieve it, generation after generation.
-- *Pearl S Buck*

Chapter One

Chapter 1:
Seeing the Promise of a Lost Generation

Just a few years ago stories about the Millennial generation filled headline after headline in the media. At 80 million strong they were the most technologically savvy and best-educated generation in history. They were supremely self-confident and had high expectations for themselves. They were going to shake up the workplace. And shake it up they did!

We first learned about the upcoming generation in the 1990s when marketers began writing about their frustrations of selling to teenagers. William Strauss and Neil Howe first wrote about the Millennials in 1991 in their book *Generations: The History of America's Future* **1** and again in 2000 with the book *Millennials Rising: The Next Great Generation.* **2** In fact, USA Today credited Strauss and Howe with coining the term "Millennials." **3**

Millions of Americans also got a look at the challenges posed by this generation on Nov. 11, 2007, when CBS News broadcast "The Millennials Are Coming" on their *60 Minutes* broadcast. Correspondent Morley Safer told his audience, "A new breed of American worker is about to attack everything you hold sacred: from giving orders, to your starched white shirt and tie. … They were raised by doting parents who told them they are special, played in little leagues with no winners or losers, or all winners. They are laden with trophies just for participating and they think your business-as-usual ethic is for the birds." **4**

> "The Millennial Generation will entirely recast the image of youth from downbeat and alienated to upbeat and engaged-with potentially seismic consequences for America."
> -- Neil Howe and William Strauss
> from *Millennials Rising*

But by then most Americans had been already introduced to the popular notion that the Millennial generation was proving to be a large number of square pegs in round holes. Much has been made about how Millennials don't mesh well with older generations and how they drove their elders to distraction. But generalizations are usually risky and more recent research is beginning to paint a clearer picture of Generation Y.

In *Millennials: Portrait of a Generation* the Pew Research Center reported their findings from ongoing surveys of Millennials taken between 2006 through 2010. They point out that:

> "Generations, like people, have personalities, and Millennials — the American teens and twenty-somethings who are making the passage into adulthood at the start of a new millennium — have begun to forge theirs: confident, self-expressive, liberal, upbeat and open to change.

They are more ethnically and racially diverse than older adults. They're less religious, less likely to have served in the military, and are on track to become the most educated generation in American history. Their entry into careers and first jobs has been badly set back by the Great Recession, but they are more upbeat than their elders about their own economic futures as well as about the overall state of the nation." 5

This is something of a contrast to conventional thinking, which suggests that Millennials tend to be self-absorbed, impatient, unrealistic, ambitious, unreliable and somewhat arrogant. To be sure, when the oldest Millennials entered the workforce in the early 2000s they frequently collided with members of three previous generations. The Millennials' seemingly unrealistic expectations, poor work ethic and impatience irritated older employees, while previous generations annoyed Millennials with their "Do it My Way" vision and weak grasp of technology. As more and more Millennials graduated college and looked for employment the trend toward workplace conflict seemed destined to last for years. Until 2008, that is, when the bottom fell out.

The "Crash" of 2008

In late 2007 and early 2008 the U.S. economy began a backwards slide that was sparked, among other things, by a significant collapse in the housing market. The result was a general drop in economic activity across the board that resulted in the bleakest labor market since the Great Depression. Estimates placed the total unemployed and underemployed workers at around 23.4 million. That translated to 12.7 million workers officially unemployed with another 8.2 million working part time (but wanting full-time jobs). In addition 2.5 million workers were so discouraged by the lack of jobs that they had actually stopped looking for work. 6

Millennials and Politics

Without a doubt the Millennial generation prove to have a very large impact upon future politics and voting patterns. The election of 2012 was the first election since 1976 in which the majority of voters from the Baby Boom generation voted for the *losing* candidate in a presidential election. According to the Washington Post, "As the Boomers age and become a smaller (but still large) percentage of the population, younger voters — who swept Obama into office in 2008 and who backed him by a 23-point margin in 2012 — will be more of the voting base." 12

The political orientation of Millennials, according to an analysis by Pew Research showed that Millennial voters are more liberal socially and more inclined to vote Democratic than Republican. But Millennials are also more likely to reject party labels, so their long-term loyalty may not be assured. 13

Into this mess stepped the Millennials. As the last workers hired at many organizations, the younger Millennials were the first to be let go. Among all unemployed and underemployed workers Millennials comprised 41 percent of the total, fully 9.5 million workers, even though as an age group they represented only 27 percent of the total labor force.

So in many ways Millennials have born a greater burden through this latest recession than older generations, a particularly bitter experience for a generation from which so much was expected. The weight of being left on the sideline just as their careers were getting launched has led many experts to call the Millennials "The Lost Generation." And like the post-World War I generation – the first to be tagged "The Lost Generation" by writer Gertrude Stein—the Millennials may be doomed to never fulfilling their early promise.

> "Youth is when you blame all your troubles on your parents; maturity is when you learn that everything is the fault of the younger generation."
> -- Harold Coffin

With so many Millennials either un- or underemployed, there is understandable frustration among those who left college seeking to begin a career. Dreams of success and personal growth have been put aside as members of Generation Y are forced to settle for minimum wage jobs with limited benefit and little prospect for future advancement. Consider a few examples of the dilemma faced by Millennials:

Joe is a 26-year-old college grad who majored in business and expected to be climbing the bottom rungs of the career ladder by now. Instead he spent several years working at a chocolate shop for barely-above minimum wages, but with few career prospects. In frustration he jumped ship to a home furnishings retailer, taking a job in its distribution center. It's not precisely the type of white collar job he anticipated finding after college, but at least he feels he has advancement opportunities at last.

Maria is a 25-year-old with bachelor's and master's degrees in nonprofit management. She has held several non-profit management positions and served on several nonprofit boards, but due to shrinking budgets her positions all withered up and went away. Frustrated with a lack of clear opportunities she decided to pursue a PhD in nonprofit management, even though her job prospects upon graduation look little better than they do today.

Bill is a 23-year-old intern in one of the "Big Four" accounting firms. He took the position right after graduating with a degree in accounting when he found few job offers coming his way. His internship initially offered the prospect of his being brought into the company on a full-time basis, but the "Great Recession" forced a freeze on hiring at most of the big accounting firms. He plugs away waiting for an invitation to join his dream company full time, but the prospect of that grows dimmer by the day.

Sidney is a 26-year-old who put his college career on hold to serve four years in the U.S. Army. Using his education benefits under the GI Bill, he is pursuing his dream of earning a bachelor's degree in Professional Writing from a liberal arts college. Unfortunately, his professors and mentors are all telling him that his job prospects upon graduation are growing increasingly slim because print media markets have been shrinking dramatically since the recession. Every day seems to bring announcements about another newspaper or magazine closing down or shrinking operations. He is thinking of switching his major to marketing, where at least there seem to be some prospects for post-graduation employment.

These are but a handful of tales, but they're reflective of the kind of frustration that greets increasing numbers of Millennials. They paint a bleak picture as it is, but looked at in broader terms the Millennials' problems may in fact be much more grim.

In July 2013, *Newsweek* published an article by Joel Kotkin detailing the woes of Generation X. "America's Screwed Generation" portrays the Millennials as severely disadvantaged, compared with Generation X or their Baby Boomer parents. 7 The article looks not only at Millennials' employment prospects, but also at the status of their overall weak financial circumstance and long-term prospects. When published in July the article quickly generated a lot of buzz as one of the most negative and depressing looks ever at the grim reality of the Millennial generation. Consider some of Kotkin's observations:

- During the "Great Recession" the median net worth of people younger than 35 fell 37 percent

- Since 2008 the percentage of the workforce younger than 25 has dropped 13.2 percent, according to the Bureau of Labor Statistics, while that of people older than 55 has risen by 7.6 percent. The US unemployment rate for people between 18 and 29 was 12 percent, nearly 50 percent above the national average.

- The average Millennial, according to Forbes, carries $12,700 in credit card and other kinds of debt. Student loans have grown consistently during the last few decades to an average of $27,000 each. Nationwide in the U.S., tuition debt is close to $1 trillion.

- Inevitably, young people are delaying their leap into adulthood. Nearly a third of people between 18 and 34 have put off marriage or having a baby due to the recession, and a quarter have moved back to their parents' homes, according to a Pew study. These decisions have helped cut the birthrate by 11 percent by 2011, while the marriage rate slumped 6.8 percent.

Sobering observations, to be sure. Yet many Millennials remain upbeat and confident about the future. All evidence suggests that the Millennials will continue striving for their share of the American dream and struggling to get ahead. And one fact is irrefutable ... the Millennials will have their chances when the rapidly aging Boomer generation begins to retire in large numbers over the next few years.

The question remains ... will they be able to assume the duties and responsibilities of the Boomers who came before them, or will they flounder under the weight of unrealistic expectations and limited personal development opportunities?

Reality Check for Today's Organizations

When my co-author, Joanne Sujansky, and I wrote about the younger generation in 2008-2009, the economic circumstances were very different. The economy was strong at that time and we were flooded with requests from our clients for help in integrating new Millennial employees into their workforce. It's a natural process for organizations to begin filling the ranks of their retiring employees with new graduates and younger workers. For most companies back then the challenge was finding ways to attract the best and brightest, bringing them on-board effectively and shaping their career path.

Intergenerational conflict was one factor that attracted many clients to our consulting services, but long-term

> **The Promise of a Generation**
> The authors of a Brookings Institution paper recently wrote: "as Millennials become an increasingly large share of the adult population and gather more and more wealth, the generation's size and unity of belief will cause seismic shifts in the nation's financial sector, shaking it to its very foundations and leading to major changes in the nation's board rooms. As Millennials become CEOs, or determine the fate of those who are, they will change the purpose and priorities of companies in order to bring their strategies into alignment with the generation's values and beliefs. 14

development of their Millennial employees is what made our book, *Keeping the Millennials: Why Companies are Losing Billions in Turnover to this Generation*, an Amazon best seller. We wrote:

"The Millennials are coming. They're well educated, skilled in technology and very self-confident. They bring with them ... high accomplishments and even higher expectations. ... Millennials will bring a new style and a new perspective to the work force, but unless organizations are willing to adapt they risk losing billions of dollars to unwanted turnover and lost productivity." 8

As Dr. Morris Massey, creator of the "What You Are Is..." video training series put it, "I love this book!!! (Keeping the Millennials). It's fresh as a breaking news flash and as fun to read as your favorite blog! Definitely rates an A+ as timely, targeted, and terrific. All managers will clearly see themselves and their employees in crisp new perspectives...and can easily latch on to precise tools to make their organization more competitive in a turbulent reality.

That statement remains true, despite the slowdown lingering from the recent Great Recession. The rate of Millennials entering the U.S. workforce is going to begin accelerating rapidly as the economy starts growing again. The 80+ million members of the Millennial generation will comprise 36 percent of the 153 million-strong US workforce by 2014. By 2020 Millennials will comprise nearly 50 percent of the US force, then projected to stand at more than 164 million people. 9

So, now that the downturn appears to be receding, employers are going to begin recruiting, hiring, training and developing the workforce of the future. Organizations will have to consider reshaping themselves to accommodate the needs, perspectives and aspirations of Millennials. And it isn't really a choice. Employers face potential huge turnover costs if they don't create Millennial-friendly workplaces.

Millennials and Narcissism
According to a 2009 NIH Study "The incidence of narcissistic personality disorder is nearly three times as high for people in their 20s as for the generation that's now 65 or older... 58 percent more college students scored higher on a narcissism scale in 2009 than in 1982." 15

To illustrate, let's assume that the average salary in a company is $50,000 per year, with the cost of turnover estimated at 50 percent of salary. In this scenario the average cost for each Millennial employee who leaves the company would be $25,000 per year. Thus, if a company employs 20,000 workers and experiences an annual turnover of 10 percent, the annual cost of turnover could run as high as $50 million, depending upon how many Millennial employees are employed and how many are leaving. Reducing turnover by just three percent would enable that company to save $35 million annually. 10

But there's an even deeper risk for organizations that turn over their Millennial employees as if they were passing through a revolving door. Employee retention and leadership development programs are, in theory, preparing the leaders of an organization's future. If the rising executives in an organization are poorly prepared, or worse yet leave, they will not be ready to enter the executive suite at some point in the future.

And that future may be sooner than you think. According to a recent survey conducted by Booz Allen Hamilton of the 2,500 largest publicly traded corporations, chief executive officers in the U.S. are entering the top spot at younger ages than ever. Right now the average beginning CEO is just 50 years old upon taking office. That means that your oldest Millennial employees could be taking over the reins of your organization as early as 2030.

But it also isn't enough for an organization to recruit and train growing numbers of Millennials. Once on board managers have to take steps to engage those Millennial employees and keep them engaged. Failure to engage employees, including Millennials, can prove to be very costly as well. The Gallup organization, which has studied the problem of employee disengagement for the past 10 years has found that only 29 percent of the U.S. workforce is actively engaged. Another 55 percent is not engaged at all and 16 percent is actively disengaged. In financial terms they estimate that disengaged employees may cost American organizations across the board as much as $350 billion per year. 11

Clearly the burden is on every organization to make renewed efforts in recruiting, orienting, training and developing Millennials in large numbers, beginning today. There may be no less at stake than the future of the entire organization!

Chapter 1 Notes

1. Strauss, W., & Howe, N. (1991). Generations: The history of America's future, 1584 to 2069 (No ed.). New York: Morrow.

2. Howe, N., & Strauss, W. (2000). Millennials rising: The next great generation /by Neil Howe and Bill Strauss ; cartoons by R.J. Matson. (No ed.). New York: Vintage Books.

3. Horovitz, B. (2012, May 4). After Gen X, Millennials, what should next generation be? USA Today.

4. Safer, M. (2007, November 8). The "Millennials" Are Coming. Retrieved May 12, 2012, from http://www.cbsnews.com/news/the-millennials-are-coming/

5. Millennials: A Portrait of Generation Next. (2010, February 24). Retrieved June 20, 2013, from http://www.pewresearch.org/millennials/

6. The Employment Situation: December 2008. (2009, January 9). Retrieved February 25, 2013, from http://www.bls.gov/news.release/archives/empsit_01092009.htm

7. Kotkin, J. (2012, July 16). Are Millennials the Screwed Generation? Retrieved May 4, 2013, from http://www.newsweek.com/are-millennials-screwed-generation-65523

8. Sujansky, J., & Reed, J. (2009). Keeping the millennials why companies are losing billions in turnover to this generation--and what to do about it (p. 2). Hoboken, N.J.: John Wiley & Sons.

9. Toosi, M. (2007, November 30). Labor Force Projections to 2016. Retrieved January 12, 2013, from http://www.bls.gov/opub/mlr/2007/11/art3full.pdf

10. Sujansky, J., & Reed, J. (2009). Keeping the millennials why companies are losing billions in turnover to this generation--and what to do about it. (p. 4). Hoboken, N.J.: John Wiley & Sons.

11. State of the American Workplace. (2013, June 11). Retrieved January 17, 2014, from http://www.gallup.com/strategicconsulting/163007/state-american-workplace.aspx

12. Bump, P. (2014, May 27). The Millennials have taken over — but don't expect politics to change just yet. Retrieved June 13, 2014, from http://www.washingtonpost.com/blogs/the-fix/wp/2014/05/27/the-millennials-have-taken-over-but-dont-expect-politics-to-change-just-yet/

13. Millennials: A Portrait of Generation Next. (2010, February 24). Retrieved June 20, 2013, from http://www.pewresearch.org/millennials/

14. Dews, F. (2014, June 2). 11 Facts about the Millennial Generation. Retrieved July 9, 2014, from http://www.brookings.edu/blogs/brookings-now/posts/2014/06/11-facts-about-the-millennial-generation

15. Stinson, Ph.D., F., Dawson, Ph.D., D., Grant, Ph.D., B., & Et al. (2008, July 1). Prevalence, Correlates, Disability, and Comorbidity of DSM-IV Narcissistic Personality Disorder: Results from the Wave 2 National Epidemiologic Survey on Alcohol and Related Conditions. June 2008. Retrieved July 1, 2014, from http://www.ncbi.nlm.nih.gov/pmc/articles/PMC2669224/#__ffn_sectitle

Strategies for Building a Millennial-Friendly Culture

The best way to attract, recruit, train and develop Millennial employees is to examine your organization's culture to determine just how "Millennial-friendly" that culture actually is. Even Millennials who have been unemployed or underemployed in recent years will be looking for the type of environment in which they can thrive. Leaders create a Millennial-friendly culture when they:

1. **Communicate the organization's vision**
    Millennials work best when they see and understand the big picture, along with their role within it. Most employees don't like to be left in the dark, of course, but Millennials directly connect their job responsibilities with the organization's success.

2. **Emphasize respect for diversity**
    The Millennials were raised on a steady diet of inclusion and diversity-sensitivity in their elementary and secondary education. They respect and understand diversity and respond well to an environment that stresses those same values.

3. **Offer challenging work utilizing employees' skills and talents**
    Contrary to the widespread belief that Millennials lack work ethic, Millennials expect to be challenged. They may not always take the initiative, considering how closely their teachers and "helicopter" parents monitored them, but they will work hard when focused and motivated.

4. **Create opportunities for career development**
    While interesting work and regular training opportunities are valued, Millennials also respond well when their career path is mapped out and they understand what they can potentially accomplish.

5. **Provide regular structured feedback**
    Whether through mentoring, job coaching or performance initiatives, feedback is the "breakfast of champions" for Millennials. They crave feedback because they received copious amounts of it from teachers and parents. They like to receive frequent feedback and respond especially well to spontaneous feedback in real time.

You May Be a Millennial ...

1. If your coworkers can tell that you're approaching their cubicles by the flapping sound of your flip-flops ... you may be a Millennial!

2. If you randomly stop by the CEO's office and tell his administrative assistant that you'd like to chat with the boss about a few of your business ideas ... you may be a Millennial!

3. If you inform your supervisor that you're going to have to leave the regular department meeting early because you have to attend a concert ... you may be a Millennial!

4. If you are standing next to a ringing office phone and one of your coworkers has to ask you to answer the phone after the ninth ring ... you may be a Millennial!

5. If you've ever attended a job interview accompanied by your mother... you may be a Millennial!

In the transmission of human culture, people always attempt
to replicate, to pass on to the next generation
the skills and values of the parents, but the attempt
always fails because cultural transmission
is geared to learning, not DNA.

-- Gregory Bateson

Chapter Two

Chapter 2:
Recognizing a New Type of Employee

From the very first time the oldest members of the Millennial generation began entering the workforce in the early 21st century, reports of a brewing generational "culture" clash began to surface. Instead of fitting smoothly and quietly into their new workplaces the Millennials seemed to possess a unique sense of self-confidence and empowerment seldom seen before. They were well educated, without question, but they seemed confident beyond their years. Instead of sitting back, learning the culture and waiting their turn, Generation Y expected to make an impact right away and became impatient when their contributions weren't immediately recognized.

By now much has been written about the 80 million-strong Millennial generation and how they differ dramatically from the generations that preceded them. Born between 1980 and 1999, the Millennials are:

Technologically Savvy – the Millennials are the first generation that grew up totally immersed in technology. They've been early adapters of social networking, smart phones, digital cameras, text messaging and numerous other forms of electronic communications. They are totally comfortable with non face-to-face interactions but often misunderstand non-verbal prompts when communicating in person.

Work to Live Mentality – Many Millennials watched their Baby Boomer parents work long hours and struggle in demanding jobs, only to face cut backs and layoffs in bad economic times. They value leading a balanced life in which their time outside the office is just as precious as the time they spend in the office.

Hungry for Feedback – Having received copious amounts of feedback from teachers, friends, parents and early employers, the Millennials embrace feedback. They want to know exactly, and often, how they are doing and where they stand, in no uncertain terms. The lack of feedback frustrates them enormously.

Collaborative – They've been taught to function well in groups and teams, partially through athletics but also through school assignments and community projects. They like to share information and expect co-workers to openly share information with them.

Extremely self-confident – Their positive belief in their own abilities is unequaled, fueled in large measure by parents and teachers who fostered their high self-confidence with lavish praise and acknowledgements. They aren't called "The Trophy Generation" for nothing!

Philanthropical – Involvement in community service was a routine expectation for Millennials through their schools, clubs and religious organizations. For many Millennials an organization's philanthropic orientation is either the "deal" breaker or maker when they seek employment.

> "And what about those ... tattoos, ear piercings and nose rings?"

The Millennial generation's sheer numbers were expected to have a monumental impact on the workplace once they began graduating from high school and college. However, employers are beginning to find that Millennials are shaking up the workplace as much by virtue of their unique characteristics as by their numbers.

Millennial style... Informal and "Aggressively" Casual

It has to be said that Millennials bring a certain unique style with them to the workplace. For many Millennials every day seems to be casual Friday. In some cases it stems from the lack of rigid dress codes throughout their educational experience. In other cases it may be that dressing down is a kind of Millennial badge of honor. Quite a few Millennials sport elaborate and exotic tattoos, for example, which they make little effort to hide or cover. For previous generations, dramatic tattoos, ear piercings, nose rings and other flamboyant displays would have been considered a type of scarlet letter.

However, as more and more Millennials take their places alongside members of Generation X and Baby Boomers they've begun to find out that there is after all something to the notion of dressing for success. In fact, national retailer Men's Wearhouse launched a television advertising campaign in 2012 targeted at young men who suddenly find themselves in a workplace that mandates the wearing of suits and ties. The commercials, however, promote the notion that the retailer's selection of suits and ties is far more hip than the products of their competitors.

Tips for Biz Casual:
- Review your customer base to determine appropriate dress to fit the circumstances
- Spell out your dress code policy
- Loosen it up when you can

However, when we're talking about the Millennial generation's aggressively casual style we're talking about much more than tattoos, jewelry, hairstyles or clothing styles. We are also talking about the ways in which Millennials expect to be able to work and interact with their fellow employees on the job. Let's start by talking about informal communication rather than using a hierarchy of communication.

As they entered the workforce, previous generations had to learn the protocols of their environment. They had to learn how to communicate up and through layers of management, including who was responsible for performing various duties and with whom they were permitted to interact with directly if they had questions or needed help. It's safe to say that most entry-level employees of the Baby Boomer generation knew well enough – or learned quickly enough – that they didn't have the prerogative of waltzing into the president's office to discuss marketing strategies.

Most organizations throughout the 20th century continued to practice a military-type style of management in which workers entered an organization at the bottom layer of the pyramid and worked their way up through the organization layer by layer until, with any luck and a great deal of persistence, they arrived at the executive suite and settled their feet under the CEO's desk.

But those were "the good old days." Corporate pyramids have generally become flatter since then. Yet it may not be readily apparent to newcomers that there are still lines of authority that can't be crossed and invisible barriers between leaders and followers in most modern organizations. For Baby Boomers and Gen Xers knowing your place was just business as usual.

Tips for Informal Communication
- Communicate Openly; don't let a lack of communication feed the grapevine
- Address rumors head on; silence can give credence to unfounded information
- Don't let gossip fester; directly address issues that give rise to rumors
- Employ social media to "redirect" informal communications
- Keep all lines of communication open to every organizational level

The Millennials, however, didn't grow up seeing things the same way. In many cases they enjoyed closer relationships with both their parents and their teachers than did earlier generations. In addition they basked in the glow of all that praise and all those trophies! So in many cases it truly isn't apparent to Millennials that they have to go through channels to speak to their managers in a familiar setting. "Chain of command?" As the Millennials might ask. "What chain of command?"

On the other hand, the Millennials' talent for collaboration may be one characteristic that will gain them praise and acknowledgement within the organizational environment. Most organizations depend upon the ability of their employees to work together as a team to solve difficult problems and seize opportunities. Teamwork is a skill set that most employees need to learn in the corporate environment. But some Baby Boomers, in particular, with their great sense of independence, drive and ambition weren't that naturally inclined toward working together. In fact, through the 1970s, 1980s and 1990s teaching team building to executives was a virtual cottage industry for consultants.

Millennials, in contrast, have plenty of experience working in groups, solving problems, tackling projects and competing on the playing field. Working together as part of a team seems to come naturally to most Millennials and they appear to have no difficulty submerging their egos for the good of the team. But that doesn't mean Millennials aren't competitive. They like to win and they also like to bask in individual achievement. Once again, think about all those awards and trophies!

But perhaps the biggest ramification of the Millennials' predilection for collaboration may be the end of the corporate pyramid. Given their preferences for direct, real-time communications and their lack of patience with bureaucracy, the Millennial generation seems poised to put an end to the traditional corporate pyramid as we have known it. Millennial's are used to instantaneous feedback. They are also used to dealing directly with peers, teachers and parents. The very idea of having to report through channels and patiently wait for communications to travel up the levels of management and back down again before decisions can be made is very frustrating for Millennials.

A flatter organization really better suits the temperament of most Millennials anyway. The ability to communicate across departmental lines, and without regards to any individual's position on the organization chart, is crucial to a Millennial employee's ability to get things done. Since early childhood they have not been inclined to think in militaristic terms or within boxes. As they begin to enter large organizations in ever-increasing numbers, Millennials are likely to find themselves attracted to companies that place less reliance upon form and function and more emphasis upon getting results ... quickly.

We can already see the trend toward flatter organizations in enterprises that have either been successful in attracting highly-creative Millennial employees, or organizations that in fact have been themselves created by Millennials. Facebook is one notable example, but even older more established organizations such as Google and Apple demonstrate the type of flat

---

Tips for Encouraging Collaboration

- Create an atmosphere of trust – Unless team members can rely upon one another they will be unable to take risks and forge partnerships

- Maintain two-way communications – too many leaders like to hear themselves talk. But if your team members don't have a voice they won't participate or contribute. Team leaders need to talk less and listen more.

- Build Upon Team Member's Strengths – It takes a diverse set of experiences and expertise to solve complex problems. Use the team's expertise to create synergy.

organization that we can expect to see more of in the future.

The "Always Connected Generation"

Much has been made in recent years of the Millennial generation's penchant for very quickly adapting new technologies. While it may have been the Baby Boomer generation and the generation that followed them -- Generation X-- that began the process of integrating high technology into business and life, it has truly been the Millennial generation that has shone a light on the future of technology.

To the Millennial generation technologies such as the personal computer, computer-based gaming, digital music, cell phones, smartphones and the explosion of apps have been nothing more than a natural evolution. Since they grew up with technologies that their parents' generation couldn't even have imagined, the Millennial generation tends to take revolutionary new communication technologies for granted. But, all of these have become a way of life for the Millennial generation.

> "The ability to communicate across departmental lines, and without regards to any individual's position on the organization chart, is crucial to a Millennial employee's ability to get things done."

Ironically, it may have seemed to many of the older generations that some of these newer technologies were frivolous and didn't really have business applicability. However if we look at the trend lines we begin to realize that a huge number of businesses have begun to adapt to communication technologies such as SMS texting, Facebook, Google+ and Twitter.

A 2012 survey conducted by the New York-based firm InSites Consulting found that 80 percent of American companies used Facebook to interact with customers. Forty-five percent of the companies surveyed also reported using Twitter, while 48 percent of those companies surveyed had a presence on Linkedin, with another 31 percent reporting use of YouTube. 1

Clearly a large number of organizations have very quickly adapted what we refer to as social media to build and maintain relationships with their customers. It only seems logical to extend that concept to using social media to similarly build and maintain relationships with (and between) their own employees.

Twitter may be one of the best examples of how a new technology can become a dominant trend, capturing the imagination and attention of millions of Millennials. Twitter is a social networking tool that allows users to send text-based messages of up to 140 characters. When Twitter was created in 2006 it very quickly gained worldwide popularity and today boasts more than 500 million registered users around the globe. Twitter is one of most visited websites on the Internet and generates more than 300 million messages (referred to as "tweets") every single day. Twitter has actually become more than just a social networking tool for individual users. Public figures, such as elected officials and celebrities, use Twitter to stay in touch with their constituents and fans. Corporations in ever-increasing numbers use Twitter to communicate with their customers and track product trends.

What may be most significant about the advent of Twitter is how quickly it grew from a simple social networking service to a vast worldwide community. Twitter has even begun to spawn its own culture, complete with distinctive patterns of behavior and a unique language all of its own. Perhaps it was inevitable, considering that the service is called "Twitter" and messages are referred to as "tweets," but many of the unique terms employed by Twitter users begin with "tw" consonants. For example, the community is sometimes referred to as the "twitosphere."

Tips for Flattening Your Organization:
- Solicit widespread agreement on goals and objectives
- Give managers authority for planning and budgeting
- Empower managers & hold them accountable
- Encourage risk-taking
- Reward results

But Twitter is neither a cartoon nor a joke. In very short order Twitter has actually become one of the dominant new forms of communication in the 21st century. Responsive and innovative organizations have already figured out that they are going to have to adapt themselves to the communication tools cherished by Millennials. As we've already noted many organizations are using Facebook and Twitter to build customer relationships and grow sales. The communication tools favored by organizations and businesses just a few years ago – email, voicemail, the Internet, intranets and blogs – are already becoming passé. Of course, we also realize that much of what we write about in this book (particularly new technologies) will also be passé in the not-so-distant future.

We have to take into consideration that there is also widespread fear that social mediums such as Twitter, which encapsulates all messages in 140 characters or less, could ultimately serve to lower the attention span of the people that use the service extensively. However a recent study by Michigan State University discovered that when Twitter is used appropriately it can engage students in learning various aspects of the curriculum. [2] For that matter, when large sales organizations use Twitter to build customer relationships their key focus is upon customer engagement. So we have to consider that despite Twitter's apparent limitations it can, in fact, be part of an engagement strategy, either for human resource departments or marketing departments.

Millennial Time Management

The advent of Twitter also suggests another characteristic that distinguishes the Millennial generation. Just like that other technology used extensively by

Millennials, text messaging, Twitter is a "real-time" communication tool. Many Millennials seem to have little patience with tools that allow users to shift time. Unlike their Baby Boomer parents, Millennials don't have a lot of patience either leaving or listening to voicemail messages. Even email, which is the most widely prevalent workplace communication tool on the planet today (with the possible exception of the telephone), is shunned by most Millennials.

The Millennials don't like to shift time. They prefer real-time interactions right now. This can obviously be face-to-face but if distance is a problem they would far prefer to either send a text message or transmit a Tweet, Instagram or Snapchat. In the same way Millennials also prefer to manage time in the here and now. One frustration with Millennials that's often expressed by teachers, parents and supervisors is the Millennials' reluctance to plan. This could take the form of simple decisions like where to go for dinner or when to meet friends after work. This could also take the form of not knowing the next step on the career ladder or even understanding proper follow-through to accomplish a specific task.

Relying upon real-time time management may make many Millennials seem to be shiftless or lazy, but it may also show willingness to keep things flexible and to consider all options before acting. This is often quite a contrast with the planned, methodical style of time management often employed by Baby Boomers. Clearly Millennial employees will need to find a happy medium between living in the here and now and planning ahead. While most organizations thrive on strategic planning Millennials tend to thrive on keeping their options open.

> A person who sends tweets is referred to as a "tweeter." Twitter users are also sometimes referred to as "tweeple." Accidentally sending the tweet to the wrong person is referred to as a "mistweet." And on occasion the volume of "twaffic" on the Twitter service becomes so large that the system crashes, which is naturally referred to as the "twitpocalypse." So, in a weird way conversations and messages on twitter can often sound like dialogue from a Warner Bros. Sylvester and Tweety cartoon!

Savvy supervisors will want to take this into consideration when managing Millennials and helping them to set long-term, strategic goals, both for themselves and for the company.

Another area in which Millennials show a preference for real-time time management is in the area of workflex. Progressive companies have long recognized that modern life tends to get pretty complicated for most employees. The old-fashioned notion of keeping employees chained to a time clock has gone out the window in favor of offering employees the ability to "flex" their work time with their personal time. Employees of all generations seem to appreciate the flexibility but supervisors are going to find workflex a key consideration when Millennials are considering the type of employer for whom they wish to work.

Doing Well By "Doing Good"

One key characteristic of the time Millennials spent in school is the amount of emphasis that was placed upon volunteering and spending time helping in the community. Whether they volunteered for food pantries, Meals on Wheels, church projects, fundraising or scout projects, among many others, Millennials possess a very clear sense of social obligation. They are highly motivated to make the world a better place. So much so that their perceptions of the organizations they work for are partially tempered by the degree to which those organizations actively support and promote charitable efforts.

Some writers refer to this as the concept of "doing well by doing good." It's the idea that all individuals and organizations have a social obligation as well as monetary obligations. The companies that Millennials considered to be the coolest are those organizations that also devote significant resources towards community and charitable efforts.

This preference for social consciousness also extends to the products that Millennials purchase. When they are aware of the charitable efforts practiced by the makers of consumer products, those are the brands they prefer. Often, they are also companies that Millennials prefer to work for.

> ### Engaging Millennials Via Social Responsibility
> - Share the Corporation's Charitable "Vision"
> - Assign Millennials to serve on corporate volunteer projects
> - Give Them Time to engage in personal social projects
> - Devote a portion of corporate contributions to each employee's favorite causes
> - Promote employees using work time for community projects 4

It's a fairly simple concept and certainly nothing new in the greater sphere of business. Organizations large and small have always practiced some form of social altruism. However, as more and more Millennials are entering the workforce, companies are finding that they attract a better class of job applicants and they maintain a more loyal clientele when the company's philosophy toward social responsibility is widely publicized.

Forbes magazine annually lists those companies that give back the most (profits) to worthy causes. In 2012 that list included Kroger supermarkets, Safeway supermarkets, Bank of America, Morgan Stanley, General Mills, Xerox and Whole Foods Market, among others. 3

Among the many benefits of practicing social consciousness on that level is the reputation it gives these organizations as being progressive, flexible and driven by ethics. This is certainly not to suggest that as a generation Millennials are any more altruistic or ethical then the generations that preceded them. But these are the organizations that a great many Millennial job candidates are going to strive to work for. These are the companies that will get the cream of the crop from each graduating class. Millennials are also certainly not above making money but they require something more from their employers in the form of a social consciousness.

Chapter 2 Notes

1. Robinson, A. (2012, June 20). Most American companies use Facebook. Louisville Business First.

2. Lytle, R. (2912, October 29). Study: Twitter Improves Student Learning in College Classrooms. Retrieved May 7, 2013, from http://www.usnews.com/education/best-colleges/articles/2012/10/29/study-twitter-improves-student-learning-in-college-classrooms

3. Adams, S. (2012, October 19). American Companies That Give Back The Most, 2012. Retrieved December 19, 2013, from http://www.forbes.com/sites/susanadams/2012/10/19/american-companies-that-give-back-the-most-2012/

4. Goudreau, J. (2013, March 7). 7 Surprising Ways To Motivate Millennial Workers. Retrieved August 23, 2014, from http://www.forbes.com/sites/jennagoudreau/2013/03/07/7-surprising-ways-to-motivate-millennial-workers/

Strategies for Onboarding Millennials

While new employees generally need to be exposed to company history, policies, programs and benefits, typical orientation programs are generally lost on Millennials. Static slide presentations and boring lectures won't tap the natural enthusiasm of new Gen Y employees or establish a sense of engagement. The most effective approach is to adapt your onboarding process to the preferred learning style of Generation Y:

- **Plan it together** – It may seem counter-intuitive to established employees, but one of the most effective way to fully engage Millennials in learning about the company and their role is to involve them in planning their own onboarding. Give them options for acquiring information or let them plan the order and sequence of their onboarding program. Or assign them to interview key existing employees and prepare a report on a specific topic related to their onboarding experience.

- **Make it visual** – The younger generation prefers to absorb information from videos, interactive web pages, infographics, smart phones and similar formats.

- **Keep it brief** – Millennials prefer sending and receiving information in short text, sound bites and capsule summaries. Keep presentations focused and to the point in order to retain Millennial's attention.

- **Automate it** – Technologies exist to make it easier and more effective for your new Millennial employees to become oriented to your organization's operations and culture. Whether the goal is to introduce them to organizational structure and functions or to impart corporate culture there are technologies that can make the process easier and more effective. Consider using Facebook, Twitter, new employee blogs or chat rooms, online video conferences, etc.

- **Make it Interactive** – Millennials are used to learning via hands-on activities and projects. The more active and interactive your programs are the more impact they will have on Millennials.

- **"Group" it** – Millennials are highly accustomed to working in teams. Giving them learning projects to tackle as a team is a great way to engage Millennials and maximize their learning opportunities.

- **Connect it** – No matter what the subject, everything from company history to policies and procedures must be directly relevant to Millennials. Make sure you help them make the connection to their present jobs or preparation for future ones.

You May Be a Gen Xer If ...

- You owned a "Walkman"

- You were considered a "Latchkey Kid."

- You understand what its like to be a member of the "boomerang" generation.

- There's a 50/50 chance your parents were divorced.

- You remember when there was music on MTV.

- Your favorite TV show was Sesame Street.

- Your favorite shoes were or are Doc Martens.

Parents often talk about the younger generation as if they didn't have anything to do with it.
                                    - Dr Haim Ginott

Chapter Three

Chapter 3:
Controlling Intergenerational Conflict

When the first members of the Millennial generation began entering the US workforce in the early 2000s, it pretty quickly became apparent that there was a "generation gap" and that conflict was going to ensue. Although the Mature generation was already on the precipice of retirement in 2000, there were still many positioned in upper management and scattered throughout the average organization. But it soon became apparent that the extremely casual, supremely self-confident, and highly-ambitious Millennials were going to butt heads with Matures, Baby Boomers and Gen Xers.

Over the past decade much has been published about the growing conflict between graduating Millennials and earlier generations already embedded in the workforce. But even with the projected retirements of the Mature generation – those who functioned well in top-down, military style, pyramidal organizational structures – Millennials were still likely to clash with the values and habits of the workaholic Baby Boomer generation and skeptical Generation X employees. The looming potential for conflict is apparent as Millennials finally begin entering the workforce in large numbers.

> **By 2020, Millennials will comprise nearly half (46%) of the U.S. labor force.**

According to the US Bureau of Labor Statistics (BLS) there were 154,316,000 people in the civilian labor force as of March 2013 (the most recent year for which full statistics were available.) Of those, the rapidly dwindling Mature generation, most of whose members are aged 65 and older, were no more than five percent of the working population. Their offspring, the Baby Boomer generation, continued to predominate the workforce with 59,893,000 workers (or 38 percent of the labor market). Generation X fell closely in line with 32 percent of the workforce, or 49,433,000 members. Meanwhile, the rising Millennial generation had managed to capture 25 percent of the labor market with 31,927,000 members.

The key thing to remember however is that all of these statistics are moving targets. The Bureau of Labor Statistics also estimated that by 2014 fully 36 percent of the US workforce will be composed of Millennials as more and more Baby Boomers begin retiring. By 2020 nearly half of all US workers (46 percent) will be Millennials while only 16 percent of the workforce will be composed of Gen Xers. 1

So, while the potential for conflict between the generations will continue to grow as the number of Millennials represented in the workforce also continues to climb, the inevitable result will be a labor market that is primarily composed of members of Generation Y, which by then will be taking over corporate board rooms and managing most of our organizations. It's a battle that the Baby Boomer generation and Generation X simply can't win. However, they must be willing to accommodate the Millennial generation in order to build high-performing teams composed of members of the three predominant generations in the workforce.

Intergenerational Conflict ... The Battle Ground Ahead

With 25 percent of the US workforce already comprised of Millennials the reports of conflict and culture clash have already made headlines. Older workers complain vociferously about the younger generation's bad attitudes and poor work habits. Although we always need to be careful about overgeneralizing, intergenerational conflict appears to be pretty certain at this point. But what are the sources of that conflict?

The Millennial generation clashes with older generations in three general areas: communication technology, work ethic and lifestyle. Let's start by looking at how technology use differs between Millennials and their predecessors.

Every generation of Americans has seen its world shaped and transformed by emerging technologies. In the early 20th century, household appliances, automobiles and radios had a profound influence upon the average American family. In the mid-20th century, air travel, television and satellite communications shaped the prevailing and emerging generations. The advent of computer technology – particularly desktop computers – spawned a tremendous revolution in how we work, communicate and play.

In some ways Baby Boomers and Generation X may be considered the pioneers of modern "high" technology, having adopted personal computers, the Internet, email and voicemail. However, technology is evolving at a rapid pace. Many of the predominant technologies of little more than just a decade ago – desktop computers, answering machines, tape recorders, CDs and DVDs players – are already becoming somewhat antiquated.

> Television, which up until recently had seen the fastest adoption rate of any new technology, grew from 40 percent of the market to 75 percent of the market in just five years. Now new technologies such as Twitter and tablet computing show signs of reaching 75 percent penetration in less than three years.

Newer technologies such as computer tablets, text messaging, smart phones, Twitter and mobile video are catching fire and being quickly adopted by the Millennial generation. In fact, many of these technologies that Millennials adopted so quickly (and sometimes take for granted) have reached wide-scale market penetration much faster than the rate at which their parents and grandparents adopted technology.

For example, it took a little more than 15 years for the telephone and electricity to grow from 40 percent of the available market to a 75 percent level of penetration. The computer, the mobile phone and the Internet required just a little more than 10 years each to grow from 40 percent of the market to 75 percent. Radio managed to achieve that feat in just a little less than 10 years. Television, which up until recently had seen the fastest adoption rate of any new technology, grew from 40 percent of the market to 75 percent of the market in just five years. Now new technologies such as Twitter and tablet computing show signs of reaching 75 percent penetration in less than three years. Smart phones had already reached 40 percent of the market in 2011 and their explosive growth may put them in position to also achieve one of the fastest technology adoption rates ever. 2

There is also a direct connection between the adoption of technology and changes in the way people prefer to communicate. This probably represents one of the biggest areas of conflict between the generations.

The Baby Boomer generation worked in organizations that were based on the traditional military-style, top-down model that had served the industrialization of America so well. But this type of organization also required a bureaucratic approach to reporting relationships and communication patterns. Traditional means of communication -- letters, reports and memos -- predominated interdepartmental communication in most organizations.

But one-on-one communication in large organizations is also important, so the telephone and voice messaging were also mainstays for interpersonal communications for Boomers and Gen Xers. In the late 1990s the rapid rise of email (really just written memos in electronic form) also became part of the mix. These are still the preferred communication tools for those two generations.

By the same token, large organizations also had a clear need to coordinate team and departmental efforts so small group meetings (and the occasional all-employee meeting) were also part of the communication landscape for Boomers and Xers. In recent years video conferencing and conferenced voice calls began also gaining a foothold.

Now, into this traditional communication landscape the Millennial generation shows up with its preferences for real-time, one-to-one communications. In lieu of small group meetings the Millennials prefer to use Facebook and Skype. In lieu of voicemail Millennials prefer text messaging and Twitter. Leave a voicemail message for a Millennial and the chances are good you'll receive a call back from someone who didn't bother listening to the actual message. Once again it's that preference for here and now, "real-time" communications instead of delayed, time-shifting messaging. Conflict between the Millennials and older generations stems from differences in how each generation prefers to use the various communication technologies available.

For Baby Boomers and Gen Xers the value of communication technology *is* the ability to time-shift and convey messages to someone who isn't available.

It's a way of maintaining productivity by "moving the ball down the field," even if the person you need to speak with isn't available. But the value of *that* seems somehow lost on Millennials, who prefer not to waste time listening to recorded messages when they can communicate with someone directly via text or instant message.

In a similar fashion Millennials are more inclined to view group meetings as a relative waste of time when the same information could be just as easily conveyed through technology. Engaging in on-the-fly messaging using SMS, Twitter, Facebook and similar technologies is generally the Millennial's first choice for communication.

To be fair, Boomers and Gen Xers deserve credit for employing plenty of technology in their day-to-day business communications. They were fairly quick to adopt the personal computer and pioneered the use of email and voicemail. The sales of cellular phones exploded at the hands of Boomers and Gen Xers. The obvious convenience of being able to stay in touch no matter where you were while out of the office is a very powerful tool set (no matter how passé the technology seems). For example, the ability to manage email communications through devices such as the Blackberry led to the rapid rise of smartphones, once again fueled by Baby Boomer and Gen Xer workers. But new technology in the hands of the Millennial generation may well transform the traditional business meeting, as we have known it.

Videoconferencing technology, for example, isn't exactly new. Enterprise-wide videoconferencing using advanced video equipment and satellite feeds first became widely available in the 1980s. But there were problems. The videoconferencing systems were expensive, not particularly portable and ultimately not very cost effective. However, when the cost of business travel began to skyrocket in the early 21st century the value of videoconferencing became more evident. What was needed was a more effective technology with wider applicability.

Early attempts at utilizing the Internet to conduct face-to-face and small group meetings across large distances proved to be primitive and unsatisfactory. Now, with extensive improvements in bandwidth and the growing capacity of the web-based tools videoconferencing and face-to-face communication is rapidly becoming more common.

Along with the adoption of web-driven, face-to-face communication tools, businesses are also increasing their use of online collaboration tools such as GoToMeeting and similar products. With their penchant for quickly adopting new technologies the Millennials are very likely to embrace computer-based, face-to-face communications in collaborative software. They already demonstrate a preference for online collaboration using tools such as Google Docs, so the transition away from face-to-face meetings and corporate travel already seems underway, along with more potential for intergenerational conflict.

Baby Boomers and Gen Xers may well cling to business meetings and conferences and could drag their feet a little as corporate travel budgets get cut in lieu of virtual meetings. But, it seems inevitable that these technologies will be just another set of toys for Millennials to master and put into regular use.

And there will always be those from all generations who believe that there's nothing like an in-person, face-to-face meeting to accomplish important objectives. And many business people will continue to prefer traveling for business meetings rather than participating in a virtual conference. But with the escalating cost of travel and worldwide concerns about the transmission of communicable diseases, videoconferencing in web-based collaboration appear to be tailor-made for the Millennial generation.

But there may be another factor driving the Millennials to rapidly adopt new technologies faster than previous generations. After all, while millions of Baby Boomers committed themselves to using personal computers and learning how to use email and voicemail, millions of other Boomers (older members of the generation for the most part) were *very* slow to adopt these new technologies.

Tips to Millennials for Thriving in the Workplace

Develop Realistic Expectations - Don't expect the world to revolve around your dreams and aspirations. You're competing with many people for a "slice of the pie" that requires patience and perseverance.

Remain Flexible - There's more than one path to success and you have to be willing to pursue numerous options. When you run into an obstacle you have to change course and pursue a new path to success.

Establish a Support Network - No single individual has all of the answers, so a support network of people with various experiences and backgrounds can prove invaluable. When you run into a roadblock or a seemingly insurmountable barrier, having friends you can tap for advice and strategies is vital for continued success.

Continue Developing Your Skills - Despite all of your training and education you won't possess all of the skills and knowledge necessary to succeed at every level. Continue seeking to develop your skills so you are ready to rise to the next level of challenges.

But technology for Millennials is more than just a set of tools ... it's more like a set of toys. When new technologies catch fire, Millennials are often the first to try them out, explore their capabilities, share them with others and find new uses. With Millennials the adoption of new technology (Twitter comes immediately to mind) can occur with breathtaking speed.

The visionary writer and philosopher Marshall McCluhan, who predicted the World Wide Web in the 1950s, coined the phrase "the medium is the message." His theory proposed that the form of a medium becomes embedded in the message itself, thus influencing how the message is perceived and understood. That may explain the tremendous growth of Twitter, which expanded by 288 million users worldwide in just the past year. With 500 million users acquired in just three years Twitter is now used by around 21 percent of the world's population!

Of course, to the Millennial generation new technologies such as Twitter have instant credibility simply because they are "cool." For that reason alone the Millennials will find unique uses and applications for the technologies that are flooding our society. It's almost impossible to imagine how these new technologies can and will transform the workplace. But it also seems likely that new communication technologies could also form a wedge between Millennials

> **Millennials are notorious for being:**
> • Overly confident of their skills, abilities and potential
> • Persistently late arriving for work or leaving early
> • Unmotivated to work hard
> • Unwilling to put in overtime
> • Unable to anticipate what needs to be done next
> • Poor time managers

and older generations, resulting in more conflict. But that's also assuming that Millennials have the work ethic necessary to put these technologies to productive use. Unfortunately the jury may still be out on that question.

A Work Ethic by Any Other Name

One of the most common complaints that managers and coworkers regularly direct against new Millennial employees is that Millennials seem to lack a work ethic. By definition "work ethic" is the belief that work is a moral good. It may seem like a generic term but according to the Miriam-Webster dictionary the term was first used in 1951. So without doubt the concept of "work ethic" is a Baby Boomer term. But what does work ethic mean in practice?

When most people talk about someone's work ethic (or lack thereof) they are generally referring to that person's attitudes towards work. We think of someone who possesses a strong work ethic as also possessing a positive attitude about putting forward his or her best efforts to get the job done. But there are also a bundle of other beliefs that Baby Boomers in particular may attach to their concept of a particular individual's work ethic, including:

- Attaching the highest priorities to the job and the employer
- Willing to sacrifice personal time or family life for work
- Demonstrating respect for authority and deference to superiors
- Adhering to organizational policies, procedures and cultural values
- Demonstrating loyalty towards the organization and fellow employees
- Practicing discretion with regards to sensitive information

Unfortunately, expectations such as these are usually not covered in employee orientations, so it isn't surprising that there's often a "disconnect" between the expectations of employers and the behavior of Millennial employees. Complaints about the Millennial generation's lack of work ethic have been so widespread that the problems have become almost legendary in weblogs, magazine articles and books. They've also created steady work for any number of human resource consultants.

Complaints about Millennials such as these are heard consistently enough to justify the perception the Millennials lack work ethic. But looked at another way, it's not that the Millennials "lack" work ethic so much as they simply don't possess their parents' work ethic.

After all, the Millennial generation grew up in a different environment than Baby Boomers, with a different reality and a different way of seeing the world. It's little wonder that they wouldn't necessarily share the same beliefs about work (or the same work habits) as their parents' generation.

The Baby Boomer generation grew up in the shadow of World War II, a period when teamwork, loyalty and cooperation were necessary to defeat Nazi Germany and the Empire of Japan. It was a monumental achievement and the values of the World War II generation were transferred to their offspring.

The Millennials actually possess a very strong work ethic ; however, it's a work ethic centered upon individual goals and achievements. This well-educated generation is very committed to getting their work done, but they may require more explicit directions and clear expectations. Give them an assignment and most of them will quickly figure out the most effective way to get the work done. And once done, if no other assignments await, they will consider the remaining time their own.

Unlike Baby Boomers, Millennials weren't necessarily taught to anticipate and see what must be done *next*. School assignments and chores were usually specific and finite. When their tasks were finished their work was done. The ability to look ahead and anticipate the next step isn't necessarily a skill that many Millennials have acquired just yet. But that doesn't mean that they can't be taught to anticipate, merely that they shouldn't be expected to anticipate without some coaching.

Many managers may find this approach to supervising these employees frustrating and suspect that their Millennials have ambition but don't want to put in the hard work necessary to get ahead. Too often it seems as if the traditional carrots of promotion and career advancement are lost on Millennials. But make no mistake, Millennials are every bit as "money motivated" as previous generations. It's just that the value money holds for Millennials relates more to their desire for fun away from the job than any desire to get ahead or grow their careers in the long run.

In this regard we can probably trace the impact of their parents' experiences. Many Millennials saw their parent's strong work ethic (or workaholic tendencies) "rewarded" by layoffs, job loss, and financial stress over the past 20 years. That may help explain why many Millennials may seem skeptical about the relative value of loyalty and hard work. If heartbreak is inevitable in the long run it may seem better just to live in the here and now.

If we reconsider the factors that drive Millennials and that sets them apart from their Baby Boomer parents we begin to see an emerging picture of how the Millennials' work ethic differs from Boomers. One of the most commonly cited sources in the conflict is the apparent lack of work ethic the Millennials bring to the job. But, as we've seen above it isn't a matter of the Millennials lacking a work ethic but that Millennials simply possess a work ethic that differs from older employees, sometimes dramatically.

For managers and other leaders it's imperative to understand this difference. The best way to avoid conflict between generations is to make sure all employees, no matter their generation, are engaged and productive. And what's good for Millennials is very often also good for older employees. Clear expectations, common goals, performance feedback, career planning and rewards for work well done are very powerful tools for all managers no matter what the generation.

Millennials tend be motivated more strongly in the present and tend to place a greater value on their free time than on time spent at the office. This is not to say that traditional "carrots" such as job titles, promotions, bonuses and raises won't serve to motivate Millennial employees. It's just to say that there may well be other means to capture the hearts and minds of Generation Y employees.

Leading a Balanced Life

One thing that clearly annoys members of previous generations is the perception the Millennials place more value on their own free time and their friends than they do on time spent at work with fellow employees. We could debate whether that's actually a rational point of view, but there's no doubt that to many older workers the Millennials' loyalty to their organization is under suspicion. But that perception may well be true and there may be a good reason for that.

As stated above, the Millennials grew up during periods of economic turmoil. A great many of them witnessed the "Dot Com" crash of the late 1990s that devastated many businesses in the tech sector. On top of that, the Great Recession that began in 2008 – the deepest economic downturn since the Great Depression of the 1930s – resulted once again in massive layoffs and record unemployment. In fact, some of those most deeply affected by the recession were recent Millennial graduates who put off beginning their dream careers. It may be that these experiences led many Millennials to the conclusion that sacrificing one's family life and free time for a job is an exercise in futility. That doesn't necessarily mean that they *don't* place some value on time at work or time spent on a specific task, just that they value that time differently.

However, Millennials may be at a disadvantage when it comes to planning and long-term thinking. This may be one of the possible side effects from an educational experience in which all their projects tended to be mapped out for them in minute detail with little room for flexibility or individual creativity.

It's also been said that Millennials in many ways were one of the most "programmed" generations in history. In addition to the heavily structured schooling they received, many Millennials were also shuttled to innumerable after-school activities. After a full day of classroom learning, many Millennials were shuttled to band practice, cheerleading, scouts, afterschool jobs, "mandatory" volunteer work, football teams, soccer teams, baseball teams and so forth. As a result many Millennials make plans that are vague and free of deadlines. Obviously these generalizations won't apply to every single Millennial but there's enough of a trend to draw a knowing laugh from many Baby Boomer parents trying to pin down their Millennial child's plans.

Tips to Tap Millennial's Work Ethic
- Give them a clear career path
- Provide detailed work rules and policies
- Communicate the parameters of specific tasks
- Explain the need for putting in overtime and going the extra mile
- Give options for follow-on actions after task completion
- Ask them to find faster, better ways to complete tasks

But this has significance for organizations that were accustomed to decades of employees who were willing to sacrifice personal time to accomplish an important corporate objective. Millennials are not likely to be quite that compliant when deadlines and project benchmarks beckon! While the older employees begin rolling up their sleeves, calling home and putting on fresh pots of coffee, their supervisors are just as likely to see Millennial employees heading for the door.

Given the difference between how Millennials and older workers prioritize and value work time versus free time, it may be difficult to avoid conflict in this area. One way of course is to ensure that you have clearly defined policies for when, how and under what circumstances things like mandatory overtime will be required. Communication is always the key to preventing conflict.

However, with Millennials, managers are going to have a harder time justifying the "investment" of overtime hours and the sacrifice of personal time. One solution that seems to be working for many organizations is implementing compensatory time policies for all employees.

Another strategy for dealing with potential conflict in work time expectations is to implement work- flex opportunities for all employees. As long as the rules are clear and specific, there's no reason that all employees, Millennials included, can't be offered opportunities to work from home from time to time. There are other strategies within the realm of flexible work that could truly help to minimize the potential for conflict with Millennial employees.

Reducing Subtle Age Discrimination in the Workplace

It seems counterintuitive to talk about age discrimination in terms of younger workers, but that may well be something that has been going on ever since Millennials began entering the workforce around the year 2000. To a large extent the concept of anti-Millennial ageism is driven by Millennials themselves who are beginning to push back against a lot of the negative publicity they've been receiving.

However, anyone who's ever worked in a large organization probably can speak to the fact that older, more veteran employees weren't always that welcoming to the new "young bucks" just joining the company. But, while a certain amount of intergenerational conflict may be inevitable, the tone of that conflict has become more strident in recent years. It was probably inevitable given the massive amount of publicity that the Millennial generation has garnered. That attention probably tends to motivate bad feelings among Baby Boomers and Gen Xers.

Savvy organizations have already discovered that one of the best ways to speed up the integration of Millennial workers into their own workforce is to implement strategies like mentoring programs, which match older workers with younger workers in a structured environment. By the same token, placing Millennials on task teams or within special problem-solving groups is also a good way to integrate them into the workforce with a minimum of conflict.

Now that the Great Recession of 2008 is finally behind us and the economy is strengthening, most organizations are opening up the doors to Millennial graduates who will finally get a foothold on the career their student loans purchased. So the path ahead for many organizations is probably going to include a certain amount of intergenerational conflict. One very effective way to prevent that conflict from sabotaging HR recruiting efforts is to make sure that incoming Millennial employees are thoughtfully integrated into the organization.

No doubt the differences in expectations and work styles of Baby Boomers, Gen Xers and Millennials will lead to a certain amount of conflict, but anticipating the problem is the best way of preventing it from ever becoming disruptive!

Chapter 3 Notes

1. State of the American Workplace. (2013, June 11). Retrieved January 17, 2014, from http://www.gallup.com/strategicconsulting/163007/state-american-workplace.aspx

2. White Paper: Employee Engagement Best Practices for Smaller Businesses. (2014, June 4). Retrieved July 15, 2014, from http://www.dalecarnegie.com/assets/1/7/smallbusiness-WP_060414.pdf

Strategies for Managing & Preventing Intergenerational Conflict

Any organization that discovers it has the seeds of generational conflict on its hands needs to take urgent action to prevent that conflict from undermining the organization's key objectives. Nothing disrupts an organization more than having groups of employees communicating and functioning at cross-purposes. Not all conflicts can be swept away with the wave of a magic wand. However solid initiatives based on sound practices can help any employer harness the full potential and productivity of each generation.

1. **Begin by revamping the organization's onboarding program for new employees** - Although they won't all be Millennials, it's hypercritical to make sure that the Millennials, most of whom have little previous organizational experience, get off to the right start. Implementing an onboarding program that utilizes technology and self-directed learning will appeal more to Millennials than listening to a 175-slide presentation.

2. **Implement a mentoring program** - Begin building bridges between valued employees from previous generations with younger employees who possess high potential. This will actually appeal as much to Millennials as it will flatter Baby Boomers and Gen Xers, whose expertise is being tapped. However it will also serve the purpose of building understanding and bridging any gaps that may exist.

3. **Tech it up** - Millennial employees for the most part should bring very high levels of competence and enthusiasm for newer technologies. Finding ways to tap their expertise, particularly in conjunction with members of Generation X and Baby Boomers, can be a very effective way to not only build teamwork but also find innovative solutions to organizational problems.

4. **Reconsider the corporation's communication patterns** - The world is changing and much of that change is being driven by technology. That's not exactly a secret, but what may be an unknown for your organization is the degree to which new technologies can be used to revamp how your employees interact with customers and how they communicate with each other. Whether you put together a cross-departmental task team or assign specific responsibilities for investigating new technologies this is a level of energy and enthusiasm that will appeal to your Millennial employees and take advantage of one of their greatest strengths.

Each generation goes further than the generation preceding it because it stands on the shoulders of that generation. You will have opportunities beyond anything we've ever known.

-- Ronald Reagan

Chapter Four

Chapter 4:
The New Definition of Engagement

There's an ongoing employee disengagement crisis in America today. Over the past 20 years employee engagement surveys have found that increasing numbers of workers are actively disengaged with their jobs. Likewise, the number of fully engaged employees continues to shrink. In short, today's workplace is not a happy place. So, when the Millennial generation begins entering the work force they are more likely to find themselves disengaged, demotivated and looking around for a new employer

Even though the root causes of employee disengagement are well understood (with the blame generally falling upon poor management) it seems that most organizations struggle to get a greater share of their workforce engaged and functioning productively. The ramifications are huge. Disengaged employees directly impact the bottom line. For one thing they have a tendency to create disengaged customers, who in turn often become ex-customers. Disengaged workers also suffer more accidents on the job and disproportionately drive-up the cost of employers' healthcare.

> Disengaged employees directly impact the bottom line. For one thing they have a tendency to create disengaged customers, who in turn often become ex-customers. Disengaged workers also suffer more accidents on the job and disproportionately drive-up the cost of employers' healthcare.

What causes employees to become disengaged from their work? The easy answer, as I stated above, is to blame their supervisors and managers. But, the specific sources of employee frustration are controllable:

- Unclear goals or lack of goals
- Insufficient resources to do the job
- Misalignment between the employee's goals and the organization's goals
- Lack of feedback
- Lack of encouragement
- Excessive criticism
- Little to no recognition

Obviously the problems are widespread and not unique to any one type of organization or industry. The causes of disengagement seem to be readily "fixable" and solutions *do* rest in the hands of most managers. Yet the problem persists year after year with little sign of change in sight.

Recent research has shown a consistent pattern in the percentages of employees who are fully engaged, partially engaged, or disengaged. Ongoing research conducted by the Gallup organization finds that only 30% of the US workforce is actively engaged in their jobs. The remaining 70% are either partially or fully disengaged. Ironically, they've also found that employees who are either at the beginning of their careers (Millennials) or at the end of their careers (Baby Boomers) are the most likely to be more engaged. Employees in the middle of their careers are the ones who seem most disaffected. However, the Millennials are also the employees who say they are most likely to leave their job within 12 months if they feel dissatisfied. 1

Strategies for Rethinking Engagement:
- Conduct an engagement survey – not a satisfaction survey.
- Cut the data by generations.
- Don't be afraid to ask the tough questions such as, "What will keep you?" or "What would cause you to leave?"
- Make sure and conduct focus groups to dig deeper into the suggestions for improvement.
- Hire outside facilitators to make sure that you create a comfortable environment for employees to speak freely and candidly.

In another study conducted by Dale Carnegie and MSW Research, the younger generation actually proved to be more engaged by 4%. Although their overall engagement figure, 29%, was consistent with Gallup's findings, they also found that 33% of the 18 to 29 age group of employees were actively engaged, the same percentage as for those aged 61 and above. 2

So in any given organization it's entirely possible that the most engaged employees are Millennials. However, the employees most likely to become discouraged and leave are also likely to be Millennials. So if your organization is like most you probably have an employee disengagement challenge on your horizon. The big question is how do you get those new Millennial employees engaged in their new jobs and looking ahead to an exciting and productive future?

Given the opportunity to jump into a job that promises to match many of their expectations, Millennials are ready and willing to be engaged. And, most importantly, they're more likely to experience higher levels of job satisfaction and would be more likely than veteran, middle-aged employees to contribute to the workplace.

Clearly it's time for managers to rethink the question of employee engagement.

The Power of Engaged Employees

Don't make the mistake of thinking that engaged employees are necessarily your happiest employees. It's entirely possible that employees with light workloads, few responsibilities, and plenty of time to socialize at work could well be your happiest people. When we talk about engaged employees we're talking about those employees who understand the big picture, who recognize their role in the company's success, and who take pride in their work. Engaged employees are usually pretty easy to spot.

Engaged employees are the workers who ...

- Put in overtime to meet an important deadline.
- Provide the most creative and innovative solutions to tough problems.
- Roll up their sleeves and put in some extra effort when the occasion calls for it.
- See exciting new opportunities and suggest ways for their organization to become more productive and successful.
- Become the "go to" employees, the core staff around which any successful workforce is built.

Tips for Engaging Baby Boomers
- Acknowledge the accomplishments, skill sets and experience of these long-term employees.
- Recognize them.
- Acknowledge the valuable insights, skills, and experiences they bring to the workplace.
- Make sure you don't overlook them
- Help them understand other generations when they become impatient towards newer, younger, less-experienced coworkers.

However, as recent research has shown, they are also probably not more than one third of any given employer's workforce. So, where do the Millennials fit into this picture? The research conducted by Dale Carnegie/MSW research revealed that the three most significant drivers of employee engagement are: 3

1. Their relationship with their immediate supervisor
2. Confidence in senior leadership
3. Pride in working for the company

Fortunately this is also consistent with what motivates Millennials. When they're considering a prospective employer they expect easy access to senior managers. They look carefully at an employer's charitable contributions and activities before deciding to come on board. They are interested in finding a career path that can take them to the top, or at least as far as they wish to go.

This doesn't mean that Millennials, like generations before them, are unwilling to compromise. During the recent recession millions of Millennials graduated college, only to find that the job of their dreams probably went up in smoke as the economy hit the skids. Many were forced to take "make do" jobs while they waited for their dream job to finally become available.

So, given the opportunity to jump into a job that promises to match many of their expectations, Millennials are ready and willing to be engaged. And, most importantly, they're more likely to experience higher levels of job satisfaction and would be more likely than veteran, middle-aged employees to contribute to the workplace.

Engagement Across the Generations

The challenge of increasing the engagement levels of an entire workforce can be daunting. Naturally, the strategies and methods that motivate and engage Millennials will differ somewhat from those that engage Gen Xers or Baby Boomers. Organizational leaders are going to have to look at the question of engaging different generations of employees differently.

Baby Boomers are, in most instances reaching the end of their careers and looking ahead to retirement. However, due to the recent recession many Boomers delayed their decision to retire out of uncertainties over the cost of living, inflation, taxes and possible (or actual) declines in their retirement funds. For this generation of employees retirement is still on the horizon and the prospects of career advancement are well behind.

As recent research has demonstrated, Generation X may in fact be the most disengaged generation of all. They are experienced and knowledgeable, but they may not have reached the level they expected to reach by this point in their lives. Many Gen Xers find themselves juggling challenges with their careers, spouses, children, and homes. They may feel themselves being pulled in different directions, including a career path that may now be stalled due to thousands of Baby Boomers who have put off retirement because of economic necessities.

Tips for Supervisors

- Clarify goals and standards of performance on a regular basis.
- Communicate how each employee contributes to the shared goals.
- Invite direct feedback and input from employees on work-related issues.
- Assign special projects that challenge and stretch employees.
- Share top-down information on the organization's performance.

Tips for Engaging GenXers

In order to motivate and inspire members of "Generation X:"

Don't "over-manage"

Gen Xers are veteran employees who have "been around the block," and more than once. They don't require close supervision, as your Millennial employees may, so leaders need to step away and challenge them to utilize their experience.

Provide opportunities for inspiration

Workers who have "been around the block" or who have "been there, done that" often find it increasingly hard to remain engaged. Give them new assignments that inspire them and motivate with new challenges. Boredom is one of the greatest de-motivators of experienced employees.

Enhance their skill sets

With ever-evolving technologies and business strategies there's a risk your Gen X employees could become stalled or out of touch. However, there are conferences and learning opportunities that can re-energize your Gen Xers and motivate them to tackle new challenges.

> **Tips for Senior Leaders**
> * Communicate a vision of success for all employees to strive for.
> * Share the goals, risks, and successes that create teamwork and enable organizations to succeed.
> * Continually communicate that everybody has a role in that effort and a stake in that success.

Give them greater control

Considering that Gen Xers were "latch-key kids" who were accustomed to fending for themselves, providing close supervision can be a turn off for these workers. Providing greater autonomy and a chance to call the shots – at least over their own activities – is a way to keep them focused and motivated.

Into this mix the Millennials are now arriving with extreme self-confidence and high expectations. More on this generation later. Let's look at the real drivers of employee engagement.

Drivers of Employee Engagement

In discussing the dilemma of how to engage large numbers of employees the chairman of the Gallup Organization, Jim Clifton, described the problem in very direct and graphic terms:

"Of the approximately 100 million people in America who hold full-time jobs, 30 million (30%) are engaged and inspired at work, so we can assume they have a great boss. At the other end of the spectrum are roughly 20 million (20%) employees who are actively disengaged. These employees, who have bosses from hell that make them miserable, roam the halls spreading discontent. The other 50 million (50%) American workers are not engaged. They're just kind of present, but not inspired by their work or their managers." 4

Based upon the ongoing research conducted by organizations such as Gallup and Dale Carnegie, we can identify three key drivers that seem to have the most significant impact on employee engagement levels: supervisory relationships, senior leadership, and organizational pride.

Tips For Tapping Creativity:

1. **Give them access to state of the art technology**
   Millennials view technology as a creative resource, so if they are encouraged to incorporate new technologies into ongoing business operations that could be a key motivator of personal performance, as well as an effective way to expand the organization's technological footprint.

2. **Encourage them to "brand themselves" through technology**
   Not so long ago organizations were banning employees from using Facebook and other social media tools at work. But now that Facebook, Twitter, Flickr, Instagram, and blogs have been recognized as powerful marketing tools it makes sense to allow employees to utilize these services to build relationships with present and prospective employers. In a sense allowing workers to brand themselves is an effective way of extending the corporate brand.

3. **Connect technology to their career path**
   Millennial employees are ambitious and actively seek a clear career path within the organization. One way to engage them and satisfy their desire for direction is to give them goals that connect their ability to employ technology, especially social networking tools, to advancement within the organization. The benefits extend both ways for organizations still pioneering the social networking landscape.

4. **Engineer creative collaboration through technology**
   Most organizations struggle to build teamwork between employees of multiple generations. One strategy that could be uniquely productive is to assign employee teams to create technology-driven projects. For example, developing a new employee orientation utilizing Avatars could comb the knowledge base of Baby Boomers as well as the technical skills of Millennials. The combined result may well help to build greater teamwork and understanding while serving the creativity of your younger employees.

One of the key factors affecting employee engagement is the relationship that workers have with their immediate supervisor and other supervisors within the workplace. But it may be too easy to lay the blame at the feet of supervisors, who themselves are often overworked, underpaid, and underappreciated.

Which brings us to the question of senior leadership. In too many organizations senior leaders are far removed from frontline employees, who rarely see them and don't really understand what those executives stand for.

Which in turn, brings us to the third piece of the puzzle… "Organizational pride." We tend to be loyal to those things that we have a direct connection with, such as our schools, sports teams, clubs, cities, states, or nations. By the same token we also like to invest a great deal of pride in the organization or company for which we work.

When we feel proud of our employers it helps to keep us focused on the mission and engaged in the task at hand. Pride is a very large element in engagement for most employees. Find an organization that has a high level of pride and you should almost invariably find an organization that also has a high level of employee engagement.

Considering the three traditional drivers of employee engagement it's clear that there is a role for leadership at every level to clarify organizational vision, establish clear goals and communicate accomplishments. Improving the engagement level of your organization may not be easy or instantaneous, but the traditional drivers of employee engagement are a roadmap to follow that can help you improve the engagement levels of all employees. However, the Millennial generation is bringing new expectations to the workplace that may require a different approach to get them fully engaged.

Engaging Millennial Employees

As more and more Millennials make their way into organizations around America and the world, many supervisors are scratching their heads trying to figure out the best way to get their new Millennial employees fully integrated into the company and engaged in their work. But Millennials pose a somewhat different challenge to managers and supervisors than their predecessors, Generation X and the Baby Boomers ever did.

Both Baby Boomers and Gen Xers were thoroughly involved in the expansion of technology throughout the workforce. For the most part both generations enjoyed access to "state-of-the-art" technologies in the form of computers, fax machines, copiers, and voicemail services. They accepted the tools they were asked to work with and generally speaking didn't own more sophisticated technologies at home than they did at work.

However, Millennials are far more accustomed to using the latest technologies both at home, as well as at school. When they arrive on the job many of them are surprised to find they are expected to work on personal computers rather than tablets and smartphones.

To be certain, American organizations are rapidly catching up with the current state of technology, even including the widespread use of social media for marketing and employee communications. But there still are many American organizations that lag behind and that's likely to be a problem for incoming Millennial employees.

Tapping Millennials Creativity

The Millennial generation may actually prove to be one of the most creative generations in American history. They grew up in an era of enormous changes, led by rapid and almost unbelievable advances in technology at every level. The personal computer led to the development of computer-generated images, which in turn led to the creation of video games that resulted in the production of computer animated feature films. And this revolution occurred within the lifespan of the Millennial generation!

A similar evolutionary process let us from the simple cell phone to smart phones, which contain more computing power than NASA used in sending astronauts from the Earth to the moon. In schools across the globe technology is used to both deliver content and measure learning outcomes. Within their lifetimes they've seen the Internet evolve from little more than informational "show and tell" webpages into fully a interactive medium for communicating and socializing.

In short, the Millennial generation has been immersed in technology, from the playground to the schoolroom to the living room. Technology drives creativity and the Millennial generation is poised to use that technology in new and unimaginably creative ways. Creativity will very likely be the Millennial generation's greatest legacy.

Given an opportunity to exercise their innate creativity and explore innovative new ways to accomplish organizational goals, the Millennials will respond with enthusiasm and energy.

The lesson seems very clear. Find ways to tap the innate creativity of your Millennial employees. You'll likely find the results to be innovative and unique, while your Millennial employee will be more highly motivated and engaged. It's a win-win all around.

> **Tips for Engaging Millennials:**
> - Tap your Millennial employees' technological prowess in working with older employees.
> - Find special projects requiring Millennials to work on strategies for integrating new technologies into the office environment, building stronger relations between Millennials and their Boomer/Gen Xer predecessors.
> - Take a hard look at those elements of the workplace that provide "fun" while also accomplishing important goals.
> - Give them as many "entrepreneurial" opportunities as possible, playing into their creativity and feelings of self-confidence.

Teaching Millennials to "Coach Up"

One of the most common frustrations that employers have with the Millennial generation is their unwillingness to abide by the chain of command. To many observers it seems as if they are disrespectful of authority or at least of authority figures. It isn't at all unusual to find new Millennial employees sharing criticisms with senior managers or offering suggestions, unsolicited, to the company president.

To Baby Boomer and Gen Xer managers, however, this level of over-famil-iarity is a sign of overconfidence, if not actual disrespect. From the Millennials' point of view, however, it's their natural right to speak up and express themselves. It's the way most of them were raised, by parents who considered them to be friends as well as offspring. And to a large extent it was also the way many of them were treated by their teachers, who played a more collaborative and less authoritative role in the classroom.

Where this becomes a problem in the workplace is when Millennial em-ployees feel free to provide feedback or offer complaints to their superiors without having the necessary skills to do so in a constructive and non-confrontational manner. After all, the mere act of offering unsolicited advice to the boss would be considered insubordinate by previous generations. The solution is to enable your Millennial employees to conduct constructive discussions with their superiors without appearing to overstep boundaries or behave disrespectfully. The short-hand term for this strategy is teaching Millennials how to "coach up."

Tips for Helping Millennials to "Coach Up"

Supervisors can help Millennial employees to develop the skills necessary for interacting with their superiors in a proper and productive manner. Besides helping younger employees communicate more effectively with their managers these skills will also pay dividends when Millennials begin to move up the corpo-rate ladder. Teach your Millennial employees how to:

1. *Employ a collaborative style* – "Coaching up" won't work if the em-ployee takes a confrontational tone or manner.

2. *Ask if it is OK to make a suggestion or ask a question* – Help them understand that employees don't always have the authority to question, criticize or challenge their bosses.

3. *State the desired outcome of the conversation* – Most supervisors will be open to the suggestion if the goal is to improve departmental opera-tions, enhance communications or grow sales.

4. *Ask open-ended questions* – The employee may not understand the big picture or all of the factors affecting the situation

5. *Take time to listen* – There may be valid reasons why something is done in a particular way and the employee should give the supervisor a chance to explain

6 *Recognize emotional reactions* – The manager may react with emotion, perhaps even anger. It's critical for the employee to not mirror those emotions to keep the discussion as neutral as possible.

7. *Offer a plan of action* – If the employee is recommending some form of change the most productive approach would be also suggest a way to implement that change.

Most organizations claim to value employee feedback and discussion. In reality tolerance for that type of open conversation is going to vary individual by individual. We don't want Millennial employees to learn the hard way that perceived "dissent" isn't tolerated or that employees don't have a voice, or are not respected. Appearances can be deceiving so it wouldn't be unusual for a Millennial employee to draw the conclusion that he or she isn't valued for making a suggestion or two or asking a few questions. The best approach is to prepare them as early as possible in their career to learn how to communicate and coach upwards.

Chapter 4 Notes

1. A Stress Snapshot. (2013, January 1). Retrieved April 12, 2014, from http://www.apa.org/news/press/releases/stress/2013/snapshot.aspx

2. Williams, T. (2013, December 16). The Hidden Costs of Workplace Stress. Retrieved April 10, 2014, from http://quickbooks.intuit.com/r/employees/the-hidden-costs-of-workplace-stress/

3. Latest Telecommuting Statistics. (2013, September 7). Retrieved February 21, 2014, from http://www.globalworkplaceanalytics.com/telecommuting-statistics

4. Latest Telecommuting Statistics. (2013, September 7). Retrieved February 21, 2014, from http://www.globalworkplaceanalytics.com/telecommuting-statistics

Strategies for Mentoring Millennials

1. **Make it mutually beneficial** - Mentoring is clearly a benefit for Millennial protégés, but there's no reason that the mentor can't benefit as well. For example, pairing a tech-challenged experienced employee with a tech-savvy Millennial can payoff for both workers. In many other respects Millennial employees have valuable experiences, skills and knowledge that a mentor can tap and benefit from.

2. **Establish concrete goals** - While mentoring is primarily a relationship, it's also a relationship with a specific purpose. Goals for learning and personal growth should be clearly established, with concrete outcomes specified. That way both the mentor and the protégé can track progress and recognize when specific goals have been met.

3. **Maintain continuous feedback** - Mentor-Protégé relationships require continual feedback to work effectively. Mentors must be prepared to give constructive feedback (even if it's negative) and protégés must be prepared to hear criticism and negative feedback. By insisting upon open communication and honest feedback the mentoring relationship will produce maximum results.

4. **Mix "hard skills" with "soft skills"** - Mentors are generally in a good position to counsel their protégés on the skills and knowledge to be successful in the organization. But the greatest impact may occur when mentors also help protégés to develop "soft skills," such as how to communicate effectively, build alliances, make career choices, and interpret office politics. This may in fact be the greatest value of mentor-protégé relationships.

5. **Build and share networks** - An experienced employee generally has spent his or her career building networks and contacts both within and outside the organization. As a "rookie" the Millennial protégé will need to learn how to build his or her own network. By sharing network contacts the Mentor can accelerate that process. Likewise, as the protégé builds a network of younger employees they can share those contacts with the mentor.

You May Be a Baby Boomer If ...

- You remember exactly where you were when you heard that John F. Kennedy was shot.

- The term "Games" meant *What's My Line*, *To Tell the Truth*, *The Dating Game* and *Password*.

- You owned a pair of Chuck Taylor's or PF Flyers.

- You remember when television consisted of just four channels ... and a test pattern!

- You owned a transistor radio.

- Your favorite childhood TV Show was *Captain Kangaroo*

I grew up in a physical world, and I speak English.
The next generation is growing up in a digital world,
and they speak social.

-- *Angela Ahrendts*

Chapter Five

Chapter 5:
Motivating Millennials with Work-Flex

Technologies that once promised to make our lives easier and save time have simply added to our stress levels. We live in a society in which everyone is always connected to everyone else through tools such as text, voicemail, email and social media. These tools constantly demand our attention, which really only adds to our stress levels. Too often the result is widespread employee burnout and lost productivity.

These problems are not unique to any single generation. However, according to an ongoing study by the American Psychological Association the Millennial generation suffers greater levels of stress than older generations. The APA says that "Younger Americans report higher average levels of stress ... and appear to experience more challenges managing their stress than older Americans." 45% of Millennials said that their stress levels have risen over the previous year versus 36% of Gen Xers and 33% of Baby Boomers. Millennials believe their stress levels will continue and many report feelings of anger, anxiousness or nervousness as a result of stress. 1

> Millennials may not yet face as many time and life demands as members of Generation X or Baby Boomers, but work-flex is also a very effective tool to motivate these employees, as well as employees of other generations.

For many organizations the solution to employee stress is to implement work-flex opportunities that enable workers to better manage the multiple demands of their complicated lives. Even though the Millennials may not yet face as many time and life demands as members of Generation X or Baby Boomers, work-flex is also a very effective tool to motivate these employees, as well as employees of other generations. The concept of work-flex has expanded from a simple tool to increase employee satisfaction to a set of very creative strategies to improve worker productivity, motivation, morale and loyalty.

The Rise of Work-Flex

Work-flex can be traced back to 1973 when Hewlett-Packard permitted employees to choose their own starting and ending times for the work day. As the practice caught on with other large organizations it also became a recruiting tool for attracting top talent.

In recent years the concept of flextime has expanded into the larger concept of work-flex. In addition to flexible starting times, which remain popular, a number of other work-flex options have proliferated.

The work-flex options available to supervisors now include:

- Compressed workweeks instead of the traditional five-day, 40-hour workweek
- Telework, which allows employees to work from home or from another location
- Job sharing, which allows two workers to collaborate and share a single job on a half-time basis

Work-flex is an effective strategy to help workers cope with and manage the complexities of life. But it is more than just motivation tool for employers, however. Work-flex is also a very effective strategy for dealing with one of the number one problems facing American organizations: work-related stress.

Workplace stress has serious implications for employers. The APA estimates that US businesses lose $300 *billion* per year through stress-related problems, such as employee absenteeism, diminished productivity, increased employee turnover, workplace conflict, and the direct costs of stress-related medical, legal and insurance fees. 2

Virtual Work ... "Rebooting" The Workplace

Work-flex is much more than just a tool to alleviate worker stress. Giving employees flexible working options is also a powerful tool to motivate employee performance, particularly for Millennial employees. Work-flex contributes to the

---

A New Kind of "Work Ethic"

As stated earlier one of the biggest complaints often expressed by older managers regarding their Millennial employees is the younger generation's apparent lack of a work ethic. The reality is that Millennials <u>have</u> a work ethic, it's just not the same work ethic often seen in Gen Xers and Baby Boomers. Like the Mature generation before them both Gen Xers and Baby Boomers viewed work as a means to achieve their long-term goals. Millennials tend to take a much shorter view of work. For Generation Y a job often means earning enough spending money to enjoy their weekends and time off work.

For many members of the Baby Boomer generation their sense of identity was very heavily tied up in the work that they did. Their work defined their status in the community and some of their most cherished values stemmed from their beliefs about the importance of work. The Millennial generation, on the other hand, tends to see work as a means to an end. Their self-concept and personal identity are not as tied up in who they work for and what they do.

Most Millennials certainly are motivated to work for many reasons but not always for the same reasons that motivated and drove the generation that preceded them.

type of open, supportive environment that builds trust between employees and supervisors. Employees who have the ability to choose the conditions of their employment are usually much more highly motivated and ultimately much happier in their positions.

A study that was conducted in England with 2000 employees demonstrated that work-flex was ultimately much more than simply an opportunity for employees to more effectively manage stress. The researchers found that employees who were permitted to work remotely one day a week reported higher levels of job satisfaction and greater loyalty to their company, as well as lower levels of stress. In a series of random interviews with

New Statistics on Telecommuting

According to a collection of studies recently compiled by INC. Magazine:

- Telecommuting has increased by over 60%. Over 2 million people now work a flexible schedule, at least part-time. 3
- Seventy-nine percent of all workers would work from home at least part-time if their companies allowed it. 4
- Slightly over half (53%) of those who work from a home office are men. 5
- Remote workers are about 20% more productive when they get to think outside the box. 6
- Telecommuters are almost twice as likely to work a longer workweek. Only 28% of office-based employees work longer than 40 hours per week, while 53% of telecommuters do so. 7
- Telecommuters save employers from $2,000-$7,000 annually on expenses such as transportation, clothes and more. Overall employers can save more than $11,000 per worker. 8

select respondents the researchers discovered that work-flex also seems to result in higher levels of productivity and longer hours spent working. While on the face of it that seems contradictory the evidence suggests that workers with greater control over their schedule were more fully engaged in their work. Being able to work remotely increased job satisfaction and led to greater efforts among those employees. 9

However, the modern concept of work-flex extends well beyond simply giving employees greater control over their work schedule. As empowering as that may be, and it is, the ability to work any time, any place, in full collaboration with coworkers is transforming the modern workplace into a new kind of virtual reality. Virtual work also encompasses all the tools and technologies that enable modern workers to overcome the barriers of time, space and distance. When we combine new technologies with the concept of work-flex we actually leverage our employees' abilities to collaborate and achieve important goals.

A recent article in *Harvard Business Review* projected that within a few years more than 1.3 billion people around the world will be working virtually. In fact, computer giant IBM already estimates that 45 percent of its approximately 400,000 contractors and employees work remotely. Some of them joke that IBM really stands for "I'm By Myself." 10

Conceptually the phenomenon of replacing office positions with remote workers is referred to as "untethering" employees from the office. Of course some managers find old habits hard to break and insist on some virtual workers showing up at the office from time to time for meetings or other events. The term "presenteeism" (which is apparently the opposite of "absenteeism") means to make an appearance at the office when you could actually be more productive working somewhere outside of the office.

> **Virtual work is a natural fit for Millennial employees, since they already possess a high degree of technical competence and a proven tendency to work collaboratively.**

Fortunately for forward-thinking supervisors virtual work is a natural fit for Millennial employees, since they already possess a high degree of technical competence and a proven tendency to work collaboratively. With the proper supervision (and within a clearly defined structure), Millennial workers are likely to be just as productive out of the office as they are in the office, as long as they are held accountable. Virtual work seems to be an inevitable trend and it represents an aspect of work-flex that could prove to be the most powerful motivator for generation Y employees.

The Time of Their Lives

If it's true that Millennials "work to live" rather than "live to work" then one of the manager's best tools to motivate and engage Millennial employees is the use of free time. But to understand this we once again have to look past the traditional concepts of the 9-to-5 workday within a Monday-to-Friday workweek. In the emerging world of virtual work we have to think in terms of a 24-hour-per-day, seven-day workweek. Within that paradigm employees will fit the requirements of their work into how they need to manage their time. Let's look at some of the work-flex options that may be available to managers and how they could be used to motivate Millennial workers:

The Compressed Workweek

Our traditional view of a five-day workweek is being challenged by employees who need more flexibility. For example, parents may be able to split the duty of dropping kids off at school and picking them up at the end of the day if they have the flexibility of picking which days of the week they work and which days they have open. A compressed workweek may allow them to work four 10-hour days, leaving one day completely open, or three 10-hour days and two five-hour days, freeing morning and afternoon time for drop-offs and pickups. This may also appeal to Millennials who like having three-day weekends.

Telework

For most employees the opportunity to work at home, at least for a portion of the week, is also a good way to help balance work-life priorities. Given the Millennial generation's skills with technology they may be particularly adept at working from a remote location productively.

Job Sharing

Although originally designed for working moms who couldn't afford to quit their jobs altogether and give up a valuable paycheck, job sharing allows two people to perform the duties and tasks of single employee but on a half-time basis. Job sharing as a concept is seeing a new resurgence as busy Millennials seek limited employment that allows them to follow other pursuits (such as a new business startup). To work effectively job sharing requires both employees to coordinate their efforts very closely and communicate effectively. There can be issues however, since the 20-hour workweek constitutes part-time employment that typically carries few, if any, benefits. But it may allow Millennial employees the perfect trade-off between paying work and free time.

Time Off

For knowledge workers projects and assignments don't necessarily fit readily into eight-hour days. It's not unusual for employees engaged in a complex project to put in late hours and the occasional weekend. Savvy supervisors managing Millennials should consider offering compensatory time off for projects that required extra efforts and longer hours. In fact, the prospect of time off, if promised ahead of the long project hours required, could serve is a powerful motivator to bring the best out in your Millennials – and employees of other generations.

Outcome-Based Scheduling

Considering their obsession with work-life balance one might think that Millennial employees are the most diligent "clock watchers" in any company. However, Millennials are as results-oriented as any other professionals. One way to gain a high degree of engagement from your Millennial employees is to offer time off as a specific reward for accomplishing an important goal. This form of "outcome-based scheduling" offers supervisors the opportunity to connect a high-value outcome to their Millennial employees' efforts. It's the most tangible way to connect rewards with results.

Results-Oriented Supervision

Because of their desire for stimulation and involvement Millennials are more likely to want to be evaluated for the quality of the work they produce and not merely for the time they put in behind the desk. Even though most organizations place a great deal of emphasis upon mission statements, management by objectives and goal setting, most employees are still measured to a large extent by the time they put in rather than by the value of the work they produce.

To certain extent this characteristic of the Millennial generation stems from their experiences in the educational system from 2000 through 2010. This decade witnessed a large number of educational reforms, such as President Bush's "No Child Left Behind" program and President Obama's "Race To The Top." Through these and other educational reforms the goal was to improve the quality of education throughout the country and prepare American students to be competitive with students from around the world, especially China and India.

In another sense Millennial students have also benefitted from a general shift away from the "Stand and Deliver" approach to learning. In that model the teacher delivered content (usually through lectures) and the students regurgitated it on some form of test. Today teachers generally challenge Millennial students to demonstrate the mastery

Work Collaboration Tools

Many websites and online services, such as the following, make collaboration as productive as in-office meetings:

- 37Signals.com - Collaboration tools
- 8apps.com - Social network and productivity applications.
- BlueTie.com - Tools for small & medium sized businesses.
- Google Docs & Spreadsheets - Collaborative documents.
- CentralDesktop.com - A work suite for project teams.
- Colligo.com - Work on projects off-line and sync them later.
- Confluence - A business wiki.
- ContactOffice.com - Groups can share documents, calendars, contacts, or files. Accessible also from mobile devices.
- Coventi.com - Share documents and invite others to edit or mark them up.
- Copperproject.com - Helps teams to share projects, tasks, and timelines.
- CrossLoop.com - Two users' computers can be connected to share desktops for collaborative work and file transfer.

of key information and skills by applying them in some tangible way. These learning experiences could have profound implications for Millennial workers.

When we give employees more control over the timing, scope and outcomes of their efforts we are more likely to get highly motivated employees who enjoy greater job satisfaction. To supervisors this could mean spending less time assigning specific tasks to a group of employees. Instead supervisors would explain the mission to a team of employees, specify the desired outcomes and allow the team to define the tasks, assign roles and create a timetable for completion.

This isn't exactly a new idea. The concept of "self-managing teams" has been around at least since the 1980s. It's a concept that didn't necessarily gain a big foothold back then, but it did demonstrate that project teams could collaborate at a very high level and produce impressive results without classical, top-down forms of leadership.

The Millennial generation is tailor-made for this type of supervisory approach. If new Millennial employees seen to lack a work ethic and appear to be unable to direct themselves it's most likely because they don't have enough experience to see the big picture, They don't understand how their role (and the role of their fellow team members) fits into the overall mission. Once they grasp those factors they'll be able to work effectively whether serving as part of the team or operating on their own. They won't be content to just sit and watch the clock while they have a chance to tackle a creative assignment and make a concrete difference for their employer.

That scenario probably seems unlikely to supervisors who think they have to tell Millennials how to spend every minute of every workday. In some cases that may be necessary, but that's not from a lack of work ethic ... it's from a *different* work ethic. Once we become attuned to the way Millennials prioritize their work and value their own contributions we will be able to unleash highly productive, extremely engaged, creative employees.

Chapter 5 Notes

1. A Stress Snapshot. (2013, January 1). Retrieved April 12, 2014, from http://www.apa.org/news/press/releases/stress/2013/snapshot.aspx

2. Williams, T. (2013, December 16). The Hidden Costs of Workplace Stress. Retrieved April 10, 2014, from http://quickbooks.intuit.com/r/employees/the-hidden-costs-of-workplace-stress/

3. Latest Telecommuting Statistics. (2013, September 7). Retrieved February 21, 2014, from http://www.globalworkplaceanalytics.com/telecommuting-statistics

4. Latest Telecommuting Statistics. (2013, September 7). Retrieved February 21, 2014, from http://www.globalworkplaceanalytics.com/telecommuting-statistics

5. Noonan, M., & Glass, J. (2012, June 5). The hard truth about telecommuting. Retrieved February 21, 2014, from http://www.bls.gov/opub/mlr/2012/06/art3full.pdf

6. Dutcher, E. (2013, February 26). New Research: What Yahoo Should Know About Good Managers and Remote Workers. Retrieved September 18, 2013, from http://blogs.hbr.org/2013/02/what-yahoo-doesnt-realize-abou/

7. Noonan, M., & Glass, J. (2012, June 5). The hard truth about telecommuting. Retrieved February 21, 2014, from http://www.bls.gov/opub/mlr/2012/06/art3full.pdf

8. Latest Telecommuting Statistics. (2013, September 7). Retrieved February 21, 2014, from http://www.globalworkplaceanalytics.com/telecommuting-statistics

9. Flexible Working and Performance. (2008, January 12). Retrieved March 21, 2013, from www.som.cranfield.ac.uk/som/dinamic-content/media/WF-DA Flex Working Report.pdf

10. Johns, T., & Grattan, L. (2013, January 1). The Third Wave of Virtual Work. Retrieved June 30, 2013, from http://hbr.org/2013/01/the-third-wave-of-virtual-work/ar/1

Strategies for Implementing Work-Flex

1. Develop a comprehensive plan

Work Flex doesn't work equally well in all organizations. Before making radical workplace changes or shaking up employee expectations it's vital for leaders to develop a comprehensive plan for implementing a Work-Flex strategy. Consideration should be given to:

- Which departments or functions benefit most from work-flex options
- Policies for making flexible work assignments in an impartial manner
- Who should be responsible for making flexible work assignments
- Productivity measures to ensure work is being done as expected
- Strategies for communication between workers and supervisors
- Training for supervisors responsible for directing flexible work

2. Start small

There's no reason to involve all employees and supervisors in the work-flex plan from the beginning. Begin with a trial period targeted at a single department or solitary function before rolling out the program to all employees. That way the organization learns what works and doesn't work, making adjustments to the plan before going all out.

3. Communicate the plan thoroughly

Communication must be a critical consideration to make sure everyone is on the same page and shares the same expectations. Be specific about roles and responsibilities and provide options for workers who choose to opt out of the program. Spell out expectations for productivity and detail means for tracking results.

4. Encourage senior management support

In most organizations work-flex represents a radical departure from the way things have been usually done. Making sure that senior management is prepared to support the program will help to "sell" skeptical supervisors and workers, thus ensuring a greater chance for success.

5. Track results and measure successes

Most work-flex programs experience both successes and failures. It's important to track what works and what doesn't in order to make ongoing improvements and course corrections. Only by monitoring results can management keep the program on track.

Each generation imagines itself to be more intelligent than the one that went before it, and wiser than the one that comes after it.

-- George Orwell

Chapter Six

Chapter 6:
Cultivating the Leaders of the Future

Whether this thought gives you cause for hope or pause for thought the Millennial generation is destined for leadership. At 80 million-strong the Millennials will comprise approximately 46% of the American workforce by the year 2020. By 2031 they will represent 75% of the global workforce. Numbers like these demand attention, and not just because of their implications for management and leadership. In addition to their role as future workers and leaders, Millennials are also going to be the consumers and voters of the future. Their impact will be profound. That's why we have to take steps right now to begin preparing Millennial employees for their future leadership obligations. 1

The oldest members of the Millennial generation, now in their early 30s, began entering the workforce in the mid-2000s. Many of them are now stepping into entry-level management positions and preparing for a career in leadership. Most organizations already have strategies in place to cultivate and develop their leaders, but particular concern about the Millennial generation is the possibility that Millennials aren't planning to enjoy a long career with any one employer. Most Millennials expect to hop from job to job, despite the fact that earlier generations (particularly Baby Boomers) consider "job hoppers" to be unreliable and disloyal.

> Most organizations already have strategies in place to cultivate and develop their leaders, but particular concern about the Millennial generation is the possibility that Millennials aren't planning to enjoy a long career with any one employer.

But for many Millennials having a track record that's punctuated by multiple positions is actually a mark of distinction. That creates a dilemma for organizations that are looking to hire and promote Millennials. Many are reluctant to take a risk or invest too much because they believe that Millennials as a group tend to lack loyalty. That may be true to a certain extent but it doesn't provide an argument for failing to prepare Millennial employees for future leadership within the organization. Those Millennials who stick it out will need to be groomed for advancement and trained to lead.

However, some Millennial employees are definitely biding their time until they can jump ship for a better job or grab an entrepreneurial opportunity to start their own business. And that's not just the dream of a handful of creative Millennials. Millennials are creating new businesses at what must surely be a record rate and many are enjoying surprising levels of success.

Fortune magazine annually lists a group of 40 entrepreneurs and leaders under the age of 40 who are making an impact in business. The 2012 crop included 16 entrepreneurs and leaders from Generation Y who are already making a big difference. The group included internationally renowned Facebook CEO Mark Zuckerberg (28 years old), Instagram's CEO Kevin Systrom (aged 28), Clara Shih (30 years old) the co-founder of Hearsay Social, Flipkart co-founder Binny Bansal (age 29) and San Francisco 49ers CEO Jed York (just 31). Clearly there are many Millennials who feel empowered enough to take the plunge and create remarkable new businesses that are thriving in what amounts to a new, Millennial-driven economy. 2

But even among those Millennials who aren't engaging in novel business startups there's a very high chance that many will become CEOs over the next two decades. The current average age of chief executive officers is 50+. As that average age begins to shrink we could be seeing Millennials taking over the reins of large organizations within the next 15 years.

As a generation the Millennials are ambitious and anxious to show that they can lead effectively. Since they will soon be getting their chance (no matter what we do now) it simply makes sense to begin developing and cultivating the leaders of our future. But what challenges and barriers are we going to face developing future managers and leaders?

Are they ready to lead?

Although most Millennials appear to be confident enough to take on leadership responsibilities, not all of them are ready for a management position just yet. Before we even suggest a promotion we have to consider whether or not Millennials are actually prepared for the challenge most supervisors face.

For starters, will rookie Millennial supervisors be able to overcome the generational tensions that persist in many workplaces? New Millennial supervisors may perceive, for example, that their older employees are unimaginative, stuck in their ways and wary of technology. On the other side of that coin Baby Boomer and Gen X subordinates may harbor the notion that Millennial supervisors don't share the same work ethic or have unreasonable expectations. There are a lot of emotions that surround the clash of generations in the workplace these days and it could become a real barrier for any Millennial employee who steps into a supervisory role.

> Even among those Millennials who aren't engaging in novel business startups there's a very high chance that many will become CEOs over the next two decades.

In addition we should ask whether Millennial supervisors will be able to employ flexible management styles? Millennials are widely regarded as having a collaborative style of working and communicating. It seems to come naturally to them and it's also the style that their teachers used in assigning project teams to work together and learning projects. But, as strange as this may sound, older employees in the workplace may not always welcome a collaborative leadership style. In some more mature hard-line industries many Boomers and GenXers are used to being told what to do, where to do it and when to do it. They may resist giving input when asked by a collaborative leader. They may perceive that leader as being weak or indecisive, instead of participatory.

It's also important to question whether or not a new Millennial supervisor will be able to think like a leader. The mindset necessary to become an effective manager is very different, in most cases, than the mindset

---

Millennials in the Workplace

- 64% of them say it's a priority for them to make the world a better place.

- 72% would like to be their own boss. But if they do have to work for a boss, 79% of them would want that boss to serve more as a coach or mentor.

- 88% prefer a collaborative work-culture rather than a competitive one.

- 74% want flexible work schedules.

- 88% want "work-life integration," (unlike "work-life balance." 3

— Jamie Gutfreund, interviewed in Forbes Magazine

---

necessary to become a successful individual contributor. Unlike most entry-level workers supervisors have to think about what's good for the workgroup as a whole, as well as what's necessary for the organization to be successful. Anything a new supervisor does, from changing work rules to setting new goals to reprimanding employees will have to be done with the big picture firmly in mind. It's a different mindset from the thinking and expectations of frontline employees, but it's a mindset that all new supervisors have to acquire to be successful.

We also need to question whether Millennials will be able to maintain the respect of their peers. This is actually not a problem unique to Millennial supervisors. Any supervisor who has been promoted from the worker bee ranks into a leadership position could have difficulty maintaining authority over employees who used to be their drinking buddies after work. And those employees may expect their former buddy to go easy on them when it comes to work rules, assignments or punishment. One of the best ways to ruin a work friendship is for one of the friends to receive a promotion.

Still, even with all these concerns it seems likely that many Millennial employees will prove to be outstanding supervisors. In heavily technology-oriented organizations the Millennial generation's familiarity with technology could be a big advantage, especially with rapidly evolving technologies. Millennials also expect enough flexibility to balance their work lives with their personal lives, so they may prioritize helping their employees to achieve balance in *their* work lives.

Another element that may contribute to Millennials becoming effective supervisors is a general desire to find meaning and inspiration in their work. After all, if they can find the link between what they do and making the world a better place they should be very effective in connecting those dots for their employees. Look for Millennial supervisors to be particularly skilled an inspiring employees.

However, before we jump to the conclusion that all Millennials are itching to climb up the corporate ladder we need to consider a report conducted by the public relations firm Zeno Group in 2013. 95% of the Millennial women questioned in their survey reported

> Develop Your Millennial's Knowledge Base By …
> * Sending them to strategic thinking or strategic planning sessions in your company or in executive education programs
> * Involving them early in the company's strategic-planning process
> * Inviting them to attend a shareholders' or board meeting

they had "no interest in leading a large organization." It seems that many of these young women were already struggling to balance the demands of home and family life with the demands of management. 4

Obviously that attitude could evolve as more Millennial woman experience success at the earliest stages of their career. But it also suggests that not all Millennials strive to get to the top of the organization or feel confident that they can do so.

Six Critical Traits Millennial Leaders Will Need

There are a number of popular conceptions and misconceptions about Millennials that may call into question their fitness for leadership. Likewise the Millennials themselves also may underrate the challenge of stepping into a leadership role. It's an axiom of life that we usually don't know what we don't know. What the Millennials don't know is that the challenge of managing is fundamentally different than the challenge of just working. In the case of the Millennials that actually requires more than just a shift in thinking. There are six critical traits that Millennials will need to embrace their leadership opportunities and overcome the reservations of older generations:

Attentiveness – Millennial's aren't always subtle. Cultural expectations and social niceties that are self-apparent to older generations seem sometimes lost on Millennials. Unfortunately there are very few handbooks that provide Millennials with insights into the proper forms of behavior, decorum, or manners in their employer's workplace.

Diplomatic Transparency – Much has been made of the fact that the Millennial generation values "transparency" more highly that preceding generations. But they also sometimes exercise bad judgment about how much they should share or how personal some boundaries should remain. This may be the result of growing up in the Internet age in which few things remain private and everybody seems to share the deepest intimacies. Young people today regularly post a ton of personal information to sites like Facebook or Instagram and similar social networking sites. They think nothing of sharing information that may be considered too personal and asking questions that may go beyond older generation's notion of propriety. Transparency is fine but it has to be tempered.

Strategic Vision – Sometimes it may seem as if Millennial employees don't understand how their position fits into the overall functioning of the company. Even though they are collaborative and like to work as part of a team that doesn't mean they necessarily understand how to think strategically or how to inspire a shared vision with their team. As they are coached to assume higher positions in the organization their employers should make it a point to draw a direct line between the organization's mission and their contributions. Wherever possible it's a great idea to solicit Millennial workers' input into where the company is going and how best it can get there.

Accountability – Personal accountability is a lesson many Millennials in the workplace need to learn. As students they were primarily responsible for their own efforts. However, as supervisors they're going to be accountable for the efforts of their employee team or the functions of an entire department.

Flexibility – We said before that flexibility is something the Millennial generation prizes when it comes to functioning in a work environment. However as leaders they are going to have to learn the necessity of adaptability.

Jumping into the Manager's Chair

It's probable that the Millennials, like the generations before them, underestimate the challenge of assuming a leadership position. Until you've walked a mile in a supervisor's shoes you can't really understand how fundamentally different it is to manage others versus managing yourself. And there's more to that than simply changing how you think. New supervisors have to change how they manage their time in order to accomplish the complex and extensive tasks that a manager faces every day.

When individual contributors step into a management position the first thing they realize is that their technical, job-related skills are suddenly far less required than their people skills. The problem is that most supervisors have a limited use for people skills until they get promoted. The equation suddenly changes from producing their best results as an individual worker to enabling the team to produce the best results collectively.

The next key objective is to review the work team's goals and discuss each team member's role in fulfilling those goals. There's no such thing as too little communication in this scenario. By discussing goals, roles and expectations the new Millennial supervisor can clearly establish his or her expectations and gain a measure of authority.

Finally, one of the biggest shifts for a new Generation Y supervisor is the realization that they *must* allocate their time differently. They'll quickly learn that there may not be enough days in the week to get everything done.

Failure Is Not an Option

The leading edge of the Millennial generation has already been stepping into entry-level leadership roles for the past several years. With Millennials comprising 50% of the workforce by 2020 it's obvious they're going to be entrenched in mid-level management positions by then, and some will begin stepping into CEO roles early. Eventually all organizations will be led by someone from the Millennial generation. We must make sure our organizations are prepared for the transition.

Ultimately the negative opinions, fears, concerns, and misperceptions of the Baby Boomers and Generation X will be irrelevant. By the time that Millennials begin moving into senior management positions in large numbers they *must* be proven, effective, successful leaders. After all ... the future depends upon it!

Chapter 6 Notes

1. Brack, J. (2012, January 1). Maximizing Millennials in the Workplace. Retrieved June 12, 2014, from http://www.kenan-flagler.unc.edu/executive-development/custom-programs/~/media/DF1C11C056874D-DA8097271A1ED48662.ashx

2. 40 Under 40. (2010, January 1). Retrieved March 21, 2013, from http://archive.fortune.com/magazines/fortune/40under40/2010/

3. Asghar, R. (2014, January 13). What Millennials Want In The Workplace (And Why You Should Start Giving It To Them). Forbes.

4. Millennial Women Chart Own Career Path, Question Professional Ambition. (2013, June 14). Retrieved May 18, 2014, from http://online.wsj.com/article/PR-CO-20130614-906047.html

Strategies for Cultivating Millennial Leaders:

1. Target young emerging leaders as soon as possible.

2. Communicate an interest in grooming them for future leadership.

3. Assign them an internal mentor or external executive coach.

4. Encourage them to join professional and networking associations.

5. Provide them time to pursue internal development opportunities and creative projects on their own.

6. Prepare emerging leaders for cross-generational interactions through diversity consulting or training opportunities.

7. Provide new Millennial supervisors with a battery of assessments to identify their leadership strengths and gaps.

8. Link newer supervisors with more senior managers and executives.

9. Incorporate a community or affinity group of Millennial emerging leaders or current supervisors.

10. Encourage Millennial groups to create wikis, group sessions, online learning and access to other internal resources for growth and development.

You May Be a Mature If ...

- You've worked for no more than one or two employers in your lifetime.

- You have to rely on your grandchildren to set up your new smartphone.

- Your favorite childhood show was Little Orphan Annie ... on the radio.

- You like to tell younger people what it was like during the "Great Depression."

- Your favorite TV show of all time was Lawrence Welk and his "Champaign Music Makers."

Few will have the greatness to bend history itself;
but each of us can work to change a small portion
of events, and in the total of all those acts will
be written the history of this generation.
                                              -- Robert F Kennedy

Chapter Seven

Chapter 7:
Empowering Your Millennials

There can be little doubt that the Millennial generation is a force with which to be reckoned. In addition to producing 80 million workers that are gradually entering the workplace, Millennials are also consumers who will \reshape how we shop, spend, invest and save. Organizations must soon embrace the transformation from a Boomer-centric workplace into a Millennial-centric workplace.

So, rather than trying to force-fit "square-peg" Millennials into round Baby-Boomer holes, we have to begin making changes that will take advantage of the Millennials' strengths and galvanize them into higher levels of creativity and productivity. Whether we wish to believe it or not this workplace transformation is coming. So leaders might as well begin Millennial-izing their workplaces beginning now. In the memorable words of the Borg from Star Trek … "resistance is futile."

In many ways the Millennial transformation of the workplace is already in progress. With the oldest members of Generation Y workers already assuming the mantle of leadership in many organizations, change is

> To "Millennial-ize" their workplaces organizations are addressing four areas:
> - Workplace culture, particularly as it affects Millennial and Boomer employees
> - The uses of technology and social media to build productivity and loyalty
> - Corporate philanthropy as a tool of engagement
> - Workplace design, especially as it pertains to office space and physical environments

already evident. Many of the most forward-thinking organizations have already begun to address issues of workplace culture and environment that engage the imaginations of Millennial employees. By taking an active approach to changing these four aspects of the workplace progressive employers are able to create an environment in which Millennials (as well as other generations) can function productively and achieve higher levels of productivity and increased job satisfaction.

Transforming Workplace Culture

Previous generations didn't necessarily impose their personal expectations on their employers. The Mature generation, for example, tended to be the type of employees who were good soldiers who fell into line and did their duty. The Baby Boomer generation, despite their reputation for being the counterculture generation, nonetheless also fell in the line did their duties. Both generations had faith in the type of top-down, "command-and-control" form of organizational culture that dominated organizations through the end of the 20th century. However, Millennial employees have a different set of expectations when it comes to organizational culture.

Generation Y expects to work in a transparent organization in which the corporation's mission, values, operations, problems and conflicts are open and known to all employees. They don't respond well to a culture in which information is kept on a need to know basis. They want to know the whys and the wherefores and they expect to have complete access to any information they want.

The idea of an open organization in which information is put on the table for all employees to see isn't particularly new. Management experts for many years have advocated strategies to help organizations build trust with employees. In recent years some organizations, such as Red Hat, have even instituted an open communications environment as a way of increasing employee motivation as well as innovation 1

However, the catchphrase in use today to describe what used to be called open management or an open organization is "transparency." Transparency means that all employees understand the organization's vital information and decision-making processes. Transparency means that workers don't have to look for hidden meanings, secret knowledge or half-truths in order to get their jobs done. It's an environment that frankly would benefit all employees, not just the Millennials. But since the Millennials are arriving in the workplace expecting to find transparency organizations are realizing that they have to make a point of transparency in order to engage Millennial employees. While it may sound complex the process of building organizational transparency really only requires a few strategies:

> **Letting Millennials Sound Off**
> Beyond regularly scheduled performance reviews and career development discussions it's also good policy for supervisors of Generation Y employees to honor their individuality by keeping them informed and asking them what they think. Millennials have opinions and they like to share them. In fact, social media is driven by opinions in the form of blogs, product reviews, chat rooms in many other places where Millennials have a chance to "sound off."

Open Your Books – The company's financials are no secret to Wall Street or your board of directors. Share the wins and losses, along with information that helps employees understand challenges to be addressed and gains the company has made, at whatever is your comfort level.

Encourage open communication – workers respond more readily when they believe that their input is actually welcomed by management. One of the best ways to reinforce this standard is to speak openly to employees about the organization's needs, challenges and successes. There simply doesn't need to be a lot of secrets in the workplace.

Involve workers in decisions and change efforts – decision-making isn't necessarily a uniquely management prerogative, although most executives believe it is. Key decisions affecting employees usually need to be carried out by employees, or at least accepted by the workforce, before they can be realized. By involving employees in assessing a problem, determining courses of action and choosing from alternate solutions, executives will find that the decisions will have a greater chance of success because they have the full support of all employees across the board.

Provide continual feedback for performance improvement – Millennial employees are not content to wait 12 months for feedback on their job performance. In the traditional model employee performance was tied directly to compensation, hence the concept of offering feedback (and raises) once per year. Millennials like feedback. <u>Lots</u> of feedback. They want to know where they stand and what they can do to improve and advance. Most supervisors should recognize that employees such as these are a "gift" and not to be taken for granted. Yes, giving feedback repeatedly can seem like a chore. But, when it contributes to the overall functioning of the department feedback-seeking employees are really a blessing and not a curse. In the same sense that your Millennial employees will seek copious amounts of feedback many may also seek reassurance about their position in the organization. Even though surveys show that many Millennials may prove to be job hoppers, that doesn't mean that they can't be cultivated for future growth. The best way to do this is by building expectations for your employees through performance coaching, work discussions and general feedback.

Tell them they have a future – Let them know that the organization does have long-term plans for them. The distance between an entry-level position and the executive suite can seem like a very long way when you're sitting in that entry-level position. The Millennials aspire to do well, receive promotions and advance towards the top of the organization. As long as they feel that the organization takes them seriously and sees them as the future, they will be more inclined to take their career potential seriously. Schedule regular discussions about career development so that your Millennial employees can see a long-term future with your organization.

Develop Them – Another way to secure Millennials' commitment to the organization is to provide them with developmental assignments. For example, rotating employees through various departments for a set period of time is a very good way not only to broaden their understanding of the organization but also to show them alternate careers. Well-rounded employees are usually workers who have had the broadest exposure to various departments, operations and divisions in the large organization. Even in a small organization Millennials can perform specific assignments to help them develop a broader understanding of the organization's various functions.

Touch Base -- Maintaining regular dialogue with your Millennial employees – a strategy as simple as conducting "touch base" discussions at regular intervals – is a good way to keep them engaged and looking for a long-term future with the organization. To many supervisors that much dialogue may smack of coddling, and perhaps in some ways it is. But it's the type of coddling the Millennials have been used to receiving from their parents and teachers so it tends to keep them focused on the task at hand and the organization's "big picture." It's a way of keeping them mindful of their impact on the organization and focused upon their career direction.

Much of the information that helps to define a culture -- information about "why" we do things a certain way as well as how we do them -- is transferred from older workers to younger workers verbally. But today's workplace is a very busy and demanding environment. There might not be adequate time for veterans to show rookies "the ropes," so savvy supervisors find ways to match older and younger workers to help facilitate the transfer of that kind of knowledge. Whether we're talking about a formal mentor/protégé program or simply encouraging informal pairings of older and younger workers, it's important to create those kinds of dialogues. Supervisor shouldn't assume that those would occur naturally.

Most supervisors have an awful lot on their plates and don't always have the luxury of thinking about something as intangible as workplace culture. Yet, when the rubber meets the road and employees have to hunker down to get a tough job done it's usually the culture of the workplace that makes that possible.

Embrace Technology and Social Media

More than anything else Millennials are defined by their immersive use of technology. Many people call them the "always connected generation." Indeed, most Millennials never seem to be too far away from their connections to others through Facebook, Instagram, Twitter and similar forms of social media platforms. Whether before work, at work or after work your Millennial employees like to feel engaged with their friends.

But, there's no reason that employers can't help their Millennial employees feel equally connected to other workers, managers or customers. The necessary technologies are many of the same social media tools that most Millennials use every day, anyway.

To begin with, Millennial-friendly organizations need to make sure they are providing their employees with top-quality hardware platforms, like notebook computers, tablets and smartphones. With the cost of technology dropping almost exponentially over the last two decades there's no reason for workers to use inferior or limited technology on the job, compared with their own personal technology.

The Internet has grown from a curiosity with limited uses to a powerful marketing tool that can connect service employees directly with customers. To achieve this synergy employers need to make sure their web presence is as dynamic, interactive and state-of-the-art as possible. The current trend is to design "responsive" websites that deliver a superior Internet experience for visitors, whether they are connecting through a computer, a tablet or a smartphone. This is important because the long-term trend indicates that customers are pulling away from keyboard-bound computers toward mobile platforms. That's the direction that your customers are probably going and it's also the direction that your Generation Y employees will expect to be going, as well.

> **Playing the Match Game**
> Another way to transform and "Millennialize" the organization's workplace culture is to bridge the generation gap by matching Millennial employees with members of Generation X or Baby Boomers. This is a very effective way of merging cultures and building a sense of team spirit among workers from different generations. Not every aspect of an organization's operations can be located in the official policies and procedures manual.

In recent years many of the more forward-thinking organizations have been deploying business-oriented social networking services to bring employees together to communicate, collaborate, solve problems and forge the workplace teams of the 21st century.

Social networking in an online platform that brings people together to connect, communicate and share. In a nutshell these services allow networks of like-minded people to either share something in common or to find common cause. Social networks can be focused on specific interests, needs or tasks or they can simply serve as a generic portal for interpersonal exchanges. The core format that permits individuals to interact with each other is the "individual profile," which provides a range of personal information that helps users to identify people with similar interests or outlooks.

The most popular social networking website is Facebook with more than 1 billion members (that's right … billion with a "B"). Facebook's younger cousin Twitter has in less than five years garnered 500 million users. Google+, which is just two years old, has registered 500 million users. In China the social networking site is Qzone, with nearly 500,000,000 members. In the business world the business-oriented social network is LinkedIn, with 200 million users worldwide.

However, one of the most dynamic business-oriented social networking services is Yammer, which was bought by Microsoft in 2012. Yammer refers to itself as an "enterprise social network" that has been designed to bring together employees, communications and information into a single source. Yammer can be used for free with limited functionality or can be purchased as a premium service with capabilities that are much more robust. The success of Yammer is demonstrated by the fact that more than 7 million users have Yammer accounts and that 85 percent of Fortune 500 businesses have adopted Yammer as a business networking solution for their employees.

In essence Yammer enables workers to improve their individual productivity by collaborating in real time on business problems, coordinating efforts and developing new opportunities. It allows employees to create "groups" that cut across time zones, geography, departments and responsibilities. Most of the organizations that have adopted Yammer find that it's a very powerful tool for getting things done in a way that would be impossible without the use of the technology.

Modern office designs incorporate:

- Less private space and more "common space" in which workers can collaborate
- Plenty of "write-on" walls to record ideas
- Warm color tones and natural materials, like real woods and genuine brick walls
- Conversation pits or casual group seating to encourage dialogue
- "Play" options, such as billiards or Ping-Pong tables to provide stress relief and help employees to regain creative energy
- Spaces where individual workers can enjoy privacy and not be disturbed

A perfect example of Yammer's brand of business-oriented social networking can be found in the experience of Red Robin, a casual dining restaurant chain with more than 450 locations, 26,000 employees and just under $1 billion in revenue. Obviously with a workforce that widely spread out around the country, the notion of bringing employees together to identify issues, solve problems or pinpoint opportunities is a considerable challenge. For that reason Red Robin adopted Yammer's service to help employees get needed support, share resources (such as recipes) and obtain feedback on changes and corporate policies.

According to Red Robin's Chris Laping, senior vice president of Business Transformation and chief information officer, the deployment of Yammer has also had surprising impacts in identifying and solving problems across restaurants and regions. When a new chain-wide menu item fell on its face with customers, a group of employees and managers brainstormed possible causes and solutions online. After four weeks a newer version of the recipe was tested and rolled out to customers. According to Laping, a process like that would have taken 12 to 18 months before Yammer. 2

Clearly, utilizing social networking tools is a great way to engage and energize Millennial employees. So rather than resisting technology, organizations need to embrace those tools that can help make their Millennial employees more creative and productive.

Social Value versus Share Value

One of the ways in which Millennials evaluate the desirability of working for a particular employer is how that organization supports charitable or philanthropic causes. This sort of "save the world" mentality can be found in the current trend towards crowdfunding, a unique wrinkle to social media that is becoming more popular. Crowdfunding is where a group of individuals pool their funds over the Internet to support the efforts of nonprofits, charities, business startups, artistic endeavors, research, innovation and related ventures. Basically the concept is that when many individuals contribute a small amount of money towards creating a larger fund they can extend their individual impact. Most charitable activities are collective efforts, but crowdfunding is unique in the sense that it uses social media to attract donors and seems to appeal particularly to Millennials who are predisposed to participate in charitable efforts.

However, when Millennial employees look at an organization's charitable profile they have a different set of expectations than their parents or grandparents might have. Corporate-centered charitable giving is not a new idea. Both the Baby Boomer generation and the Mature generation before them were very attuned to the idea of being involved in corporate charitable giving programs. As far back as the 19th century there were groups who organized "Community Chest" campaigns to involve both employers and employees in forming a fund that could be plowed back into the community for worthy causes. In the 20th century, Community Chest campaigns generally evolved into the Baby Boomer's favorite

Crowdfunding Sites for Non-Profits

1. StartSomeGood.com is great for early-stage social good projects that are not (yet) 501(c)(3) registered nonprofits.

2. Rockethub.com: A broad platform targeting "artists, scientists, entrepreneurs, and philanthropists,

3. Causes.com: Designed specifically for 501(c)(3) registered nonprofits to raise money.

4. Razoo.com: Razoo boasts that it has now helped 14,000 causes raise over $100 million. This site is exclusively for social good causes but is not limited to 501(c)(3).

5. Crowdrise.com: Crowdrise is a site for 501(c)(3) charities to raise money, with the novelty being that anyone can sign up to volunteer to launch a fundraising campaign for a charity already registered on the site.

Source: Forbes 7

charities, such as the United Way and local blood drives. So giving to charitable causes at work was not uncommon to older generations.

However the Millennials don't take the same "pledge card charity" approach that their predecessors did. Millennial employees have higher expectations when it comes to corporate-based charitable giving. For example, many Millennials question the logic of relegating matching charitable contributions to a single campaign during a single season of the year. They are much more oriented towards

> **Millennials don't see work as a location, they tend to view work as a function.**

matching contributions being offered to employees throughout the entire year. But there's also a hands-on component to the Millennial's preference for charitable contributions.

Organizations that tend to attract the interest of Millennial workers are often organizations that make time for employees to engage in volunteer activities during the workday, with paid time off to participate. Some organizations have even encouraged employees to locate local worthy causes so they can engage in a volunteer day, during which an employee group performs physical work or fundraising efforts for the selected charity. Some of the most progressive organizations even go so far as to offer financial grants derived from profit margins to their employees' favorite charities.

Through these initiatives organizations are responding to the Millennials' inclination to influence the greater world around themselves through their own employment. Employers who are looking to improve employee engagement could actually initiate no better strategy then to engage employees in sound social causes and volunteer opportunities.

Replace "Cubicle Farms" with "Millennial Spaces"

The rise of the Millennial generation is coinciding with the demise of the most common office configurations of the previous generation. When the Baby Boomers began flowing into the workforce in the 1960s and early 1970s, organizations replaced those desk-filled open offices common though the 1950s with individual cubicles. Cubicles seemed to provide workers with more privacy and a degree of personalization while supposedly promoting greater collaboration. But office workers soon came to resent the "cubicle farms" that dominated most workplaces and also became the butt of numerous jokes in Dilbert cartoons.

But, the office environment of the Millennial generation is going to be something quite different from the cubicle-oriented environment of previous generations. Cubicles presume that knowledge workers require certain basics to be productive, such as a computer, a telephone, desk space, horizontal work surfaces, file storage, an office chair and a minimal level of privacy. In reality technology has transformed our traditional office spaces into totally portable devices that generally serve all the same functions that were provided for in office cubicles. Armed with technology in the form of notebook computers, tablets and smartphones, modern office workers can literally carry their office with them wherever they wish to go to perform work.

Work certainly can be conducted in office environment, as need be, but it can also be conducted in coffee shops, at home, while traveling, at poolside and virtually anywhere else workers care to be. Modern designers are attempting to develop office spaces that acknowledge this reality while also recognizing the need for face-to-face communications. Many are beginning to adapt their designs to the needs of Millennials in very innovative ways. The types of workspaces that appeal most to the Millennial generation would seem to be a combination of office, coffee shop and living room. In some cases designers also incorporate some elements of gaming into their office designs.

One of the differences between Millennials and older generations is that Generation Y has a tendency to blend work life with home life. As a result their preferred office environment should feel more "residential" than "business." This also suggests that Millennials hold a very different definition of work than older generations. Millennials don't typically view work simply as a place where they have to "put in time."

An interesting example of this approach to workplace design can be found in the offices of Red Frog Events, a Chicago-based marketing firm. Red Frog's space is large, open, flexible and highly collaborative. The working space includes creative touches such as artificial tree houses, an indoor slide and a conference table constructed entirely of Legos. In addition to some of the typical perks, Red

---

Adapting a Millennial Mindset

Jeanne Meister, writing in *Forbes* magazine, suggests that Gen Xers and Baby Boomers ought to consider adopting a "Millennial mindset." Her recommendations (which are based on the Pew Research Center's ongoing study of the Millennial generation) include the following suggestions: 5

Play social games on the Internet or your smartphone

Consider watching less television. Forty-three percent of Millennials don't watch as much as one hour of television per day. But they spend considerably more time playing social games daily.

Build "social" (media) into your life

Millennials often take to the keypad to type out texts to their buddies, update their Facebook status and send Tweets to the entire Internet. The average Millennial sends around 20 texts per day while 41 percent of adults overall (including most Baby Boomers) don't send *any* text messages at all. 6

Frog employees can also enjoy a game of foosball or take a ride on the company's indoor zip line. And on Fridays, after a long and intense work week, employees can knock off and enjoy a beer or two at the company's in-house bar. 3

Another example of a distinctively innovative workplace is the offices of Pittsburgh-based MAYA Design, a design consultancy and technology research lab. Their office is designed to foster innovation and promote creativity, which is the company's bread and butter. Much of their office design features round walls and circular meeting spaces, rather than the conventional straight lines of rectangular board rooms. Large amounts of wall space are devoted to whiteboards that can serve as blank canvases for employees' ideas.

In various parts of the office employee desks are arranged into wall-less interdisciplinary "neighborhoods" to encourage greater collaboration across project teams. The offices main "ideation" space is called Kiva®, which is a Native American term for circular meeting rooms that served as gathering places for special events. These workspaces include completely wraparound whiteboards for instant collaboration and as a way to capture the evolution of creative concepts. 4

Millennial-friendly offices such as Red Frog's and MAYA's are also located in urban settings, which tend to be much more attractive to

> **Millennials can build a solid reputation by:**
> - Speaking diplomatically & with tact
> - Using good sense
> - Judging the repercussions of actions before acting … or speaking
> - Accommodating the viewpoints of subordinates and superiors
> - Making allowances for other people's needs, problems, and priorities

Millennials then the sprawling suburban office parks that previously attracted the Baby Boomer generation. But we must remember that the key to "Millennial-izing" an organization's workspace is about much more than simply attracting and retaining Generation Y employees. It's also about inspiring employees to deliver their best, most innovative contributions to the bottom line.

Learning To Think Like A Millennial

Change is always challenging. For Boomers and Gen Xers adapting to the upcoming Millennial generation could prove to be a troubling process. We have to recognize that the realities that formed us when we were students will tend to shape our mindsets and thinking as adults. The challenge is that we can't allow our experiences and perceptions to "calcify" and prevent us from looking at the world through the lens of a new, upcoming generation. There could be much to be gained in understanding the Millennial mindset as more members of this generation take their places as workers and consumers.

Thinking like a Millennial is in fact a constructive way to anticipate how an organization can begin the process of adapting to the highly dynamic work style of the next generation. There seems to be little doubt that Millennials are going to transform the workplace and that they are already having a significant impact upon how we get things done. As employees the Millennial generation is a tidal force that is either going to swamp our organizations or lift them to higher levels of productivity and effectiveness. For Baby Boomers it may simply be a matter of "sink or swim."

Chapter 7 Notes

1. Whitehurst, J. (2012, May 14). How My Company Made Truly Open Management Work. Retrieved January 12, 2014, from http://www.forbes.com/sites/forbesleadershipforum/2012/05/14/how-my-company-made-truly-open-management-work/

2. Fiorletta, A. (2013, July 24). Red Robin Empowers Millennial Employees With Social Enterprise Solutions. Retrieved May 5, 2014, from http://www.retailtouchpoints.com/in-store-insights/2730-red-robin-empowers-millennial-employees-with-social-enterprise-solutions

3. Kalman, F. (2012, March 20). How to 'Millennialize' the Office. Retrieved April 29, 2013, from http://talentmgt.com/articles/how-to-millennialize-the-office

4. Company | MAYA Design. (2014, January 1). Retrieved May 13, 2014, from http://maya.com/company

5. Meister, J. (2012, October 5). Three Reasons You Need To Adopt A Millennial Mindset Regardless Of Your Age. Retrieved June 14, 2014, from http://www.forbes.com/sites/jeannemeister/2012/10/05/millennialmindse/

6. Meister, J. (2012, October 5). Three Reasons You Need To Adopt A Millennial Mindset Regardless Of Your Age. Retrieved June 14, 2014, from http://www.forbes.com/sites/jeannemeister/2012/10/05/millennialmindse/

7. Barnett, C. (2013, May 8). Top 10 Crowdfunding Sites For Fundraising. Retrieved April 15, 2014, from http://www.forbes.com/sites/chancebarnett/2013/05/08/top-10-crowdfunding-sites-for-fundraising/

Empowerment Strategies for Millennials

1. Develop interpersonal skills by:

- Asking questions politely
- Keeping a sharp eye out for patterns and trends (such as dress codes)
- Listening carefully to how employees speak with each other in the workplace
- Learning to role play tough supervisory situations through workshops
- Learning etiquette and client relations through "hands on" experiences

2. Develop performance management skills by:

- Setting standards and measures of performance and evaluating employee's efforts against those standards
- Providing feedback to employees for improvement
- Address performance problems and explore multiple options

3. Get off to a strong supervisory start by:

- Engaging in two-way communications with each employee
- Conducting a series of one-on-one discussions with each employee to become acquainted and discuss expectations
- Answering the question "What will remain the same and what's going to change?" for each direct report
- Making sure that employees understand the meaning of success
- Establishing a productive working relationship with each employee
- Celebrating all successes, big and small
- Learning proficiency in performing your own duties and administrative tasks
- Submitting timely reports and using technology to do them faster and better

---

The philosophy of the schoolroom in one generation will be the philosophy of government in the next.

-- Abraham Lincoln

Chapter Eight

Chapter 8:
Millennials in the Real World

How the Millennial generation will ultimately impact the world is, at this stage, equal parts conjecture and experience. When we're talking about an entire generation with millions of members we obviously have to deal to a certain extent in generalities. But even then the realities are startling enough. What we know for certain is this... the Millennials grew up in a world that was changing at blistering speed, with bewildering technologies and stunning new realities.

Millennials experienced the world differently than did the Boomers, Gen Xers and Matures before them, so differences in perceptions and values had to be inevitable. However, we need to distinguish between realities and stereotypes. Members of all generations in the workplace have the potential to move past the stereotypes and forge powerful new bonds of collaboration with Millennials. But first we need to shed some of the myths and stereotypes that color those older generations' impressions of Generation Y.

So much has been written and said by Baby Boomers about the Millennial generation that it could be easy to see certain sinister motives behind their viewpoints. As has often been pointed out, Boomers tend to see Millennial employees as "spoiled, lazy, and entitled." In contrast, Millennials themselves tend to see their generation as "tech savvy, tuned in, and cool."

Once again we're dealing with broad generalizations, and yet the perceptions are so persistent that a recent *Time Magazine* cover story tagged Millennials as the "Me, Me, Me" generation. Those are the surface perceptions that we touched upon in previous chapters. But if we dig beneath that stereotype we begin to see that the reality is rather more complex than that.

Millennials and Materialism

"The millennials have developed a reputation for a certain materialism. In a Pew Research Center survey in which different generations were asked what made them unique, Baby Boomers responded with qualities like "work ethic"; millennials offered "clothes." But, according to new data, even though the recession is over, this generation is not looking to gorge; instead, they are the kind of hungry that cannot stop thinking about food. "Call it materialism if you want," said Neil Howe, an author of the 1991 book "Generations." It seems more like financial melancholy. "They look at the house their parents live in and say, 'I could work for 100 years and I couldn't afford this place,' " Howe said.

-- By Annie Lowrey from "Do Millennials Stand a Chance in the Real World?" New York Times Magazine 8

Millennials are not just a product of the times or their technologies. They've obviously been heavily influenced by their technology as well as their education, but parenting is often blamed for the Millennials' unreasonable expectations and poor work ethic. Many people believe it has a lot to do with all those hovering "helicopter" parents armed with so many trophies and awards.

But Millennials are growing tired of being pigeonholed and labeled in the same ways over and over again. There seems to be a growing pushback by Millennials who feel they're getting a bad rap. The new mantra seems to be "if you don't like us then you have to blame yourselves… because you made us this way." In fact, there may be a certain amount of truth to that. A recent article by Millennial writer Noreen Malone published in *New York Magazine* addresses the question of how Generation Y came to be, well … so very Millennial. She writes:

Human Networks vs. Social Networks

Ashley Crouch, writing in the *Huffington Post*, advised Millennials to "Stop counting your Facebook friends and start making real friends. Neuroscientists report that humans are biologically wired to form strong social communities in order to truly flourish. Yet in recent history, authentic communities have been dissolving in favor of a digital individualism. Buck the trend by calling a different friend every week -- for example, during a lunch hour or on your way home from happy hour with the colleagues. You'll like your physical friendships even more than your Facebook ones." 4

"Our generation is the product of two long-term social experiments conducted by our parents. The first sought to create little hyper-achievers encouraged to explore our interests and talents, so long as that could be spun for maximum effect on a college application. (I would like to take this forum to at last admit that my co-secretaryship of the math club had nothing to do with any passion for numbers and much to do with the extra-credit points.) In the second experiment, which was a reaction to their own distant moms and dads, our parents tried to see how much self-confidence they could pack into us, like so many overstuffed microfiber love seats, and accordingly we were awarded clip-art Certificates of Participation just for showing up." 1

Perhaps in many ways the best generalization of all is to recognize that all generalizations are suspect, especially generalizations made about Generation Y.

Working Beyond the Stereotypes

Leaders who have the challenge of managing Millennials will need to put aside stereotypes, myths and assumptions if they are going to be successful motivating and engaging their youngest employees. After all, whatever generational biases or viewpoints they might hold about Millennials, managers still have to recognize that each of their Millennial employees is an individual, with unique needs, distinct perceptions and singular ambitions. Building rapport with Millennials and engaging them at work is going to require a strategic approach. The Millennials' supervisors are advised to implement the following strategies:

Withhold assumptions - Get to know your new, young worker before lumping him or her into the same category as all other Millennials.

Shake off the stereotypes - If you keep an open mind you are likely to be surprised by the quality of effort that Millennials will produce.

Encourage open communication – Millennials respond best when communication is direct, honest and without hidden agendas. The quickest way to lose the loyalty of Millennials is to withhold information or restrict it to a select few individuals.

Give negative feedback with discretion – Millennial employees are going to make mistakes. However, any negative feedback that has to be delivered as a result of those mistakes should be done in private, at the proper time, using the proper channels. The worst mistake would be to single out Millennial employees for shame or public disapproval.

Provide direct and sincere positive feedback – It has often been pointed out that Millennials are accustomed to copious amounts of feedback and relish receiving input on their performances and accomplishments. Acknowledging the accomplishments of your Millennial employees is a critical element in their sense of loyalty to the organization and commitment to a long-term career path.

Of course, it's possible for anybody dealing with members of different generations to fall into the trap of believing myths, rumors or stereotypes. There have always been clashes between different generations as long as there have been humans walking the earth. Aristotle, for example, wrote more than 2,000 years ago about how frustrating he found students to be!

Several decades ago a marketing professor at the University of Colorado produced a landmark book and presentation on the subject of dealing with different generations. Dr. Morris Massey wrote an insightful book and film series titled *What You Are Is Where*

Aristotle on Youth

"Our youth now love luxury. They have bad manners, contempt for authority; they show disrespect for their elders and love chatter in place of exercise; they no longer rise when elders enter the room; they contradict their parents, chatter before company; gobble up their food and tyrannize their teachers."

-- Circa 320 BC

You Were When. His seminal works "schooled" the Mature and Baby Boomer generations in how they needed to deal with each other. Several years later Massey issued a follow-up volume called *What You Are Is Where You Were When...* *AGAIN!* 2

Massey's advice on how best to deal with members of different generations fell into four distinct recommendations:

- Ask people... and listen to what they say
- Look objectively and nonjudgmentally at other people
- Accept that other people's values are just as valid as your own
- Put your own values on "hold"

For some reason human beings seem to have an innate tendency to cling to their values and defend them in the face of apparent contradictions from others. Massey is correct in pointing out that another person's values may simply be different without being either wrong or threatening in any way.

Helping Millennials Thrive in the "Real World"

All employees take up their positions with certain expectations, hopes and dreams. However, reality has a way of tempering every employee's expectations. For example, in previous generations many individuals prided themselves on having learned at the "school of hard knocks." You don't hear this phrase as much anymore, at least partially because formal college education is considered to be somewhat superior to learning on the job, in the trenches or on the streets.

To put it another way, "bootstrapping" (the task of pulling oneself upward by one's own boots) is no longer a practical approach in a fast-moving, high-tech world. Today's employees need to build on their formal, structured education with practical experiences in the world and the workplace. That means starting at the bottom (usually) and climbing the corporate ladder rung by rung. There certainly might be shortcuts, such as starting a new enterprise from scratch, but in reality the surest way to succeed is step-by-step, one position of the time, inching towards the top, making mistakes along the way, and reaching the senior executive suite after a lengthy, loyal service to one employer.

Unfortunately, that traditional career path

Millennials and Persistence

Millennials need to understand that persistence pays off. Entrepreneur and inventor James Dyson created his first successful cyclone vacuum cleaner in 1993. But that accomplishment was the result of creating more than 5,126 failed prototypes over a 15-year period. However, his invention revolutionized the vacuum cleaner industry. Dyson recently said, "Failure is interesting -- it's part of making progress. You never learn from success, but you do learn from failure. I started out with a simple idea, and by the end, it got more audacious and interesting. I got to a place I never could have imagined because I learned what worked and didn't work." 5

might not be realistic in today's world. Millennial graduates continue to face difficulty finding a job following the recession of 2008. The economy has rebounded since and employers are hiring in larger numbers than before, yet competition is fierce and many Millennials still struggle to grab onto the first rung of the career ladder.

But when those career opportunities *do* finally present themselves, how prepared will Millennials be to actually take advantage of them? Unfortunately Generation Y may be less prepared to thrive in the real world, in part because so many of them may have unrealistic expectations about life and work. Their experiences in school won't necessarily translate into the social skills necessary to function productively on the job. The culture of education is not necessarily a parallel to the culture of business.

> **Millennials and Humility**
> College Basketball Coach Rick Pitino says, "Humility is the true key to success. Successful people lose their way at times. ... Humble people share the credit and wealth, remaining focused and hungry to continue the journey of success." 6

Millennials will most likely find that their bosses won't leave detailed instructions in writing or provide continual feedback on performance through grades and report cards. They might not understand that the consequences of failure in the working world might not be a "do over." And they'll have to learn that the relatively "flat" hierarchy of a school is vastly different than the typical hierarchy of a large corporation.

In many cases it might be the Millennials' strengths that will sabotage them in the workplace. We generally believe that strengths are things that an individual does well, and we consider weaknesses as things that an individual either does poorly or cannot do at all. However, it's also not uncommon for some of our strengths to become weaknesses when we overuse them or use them inappropriately.

For example, people who are gifted at analysis may become so bogged down in data that they fail to take action. People who are decisive can sabotage themselves if they take action before having all the data. Gifted talkers can become annoying if they talk too much. But skilled listeners may also annoy others by refusing to speak up when necessary. Each of us carries within ourselves the keys to both success and failure.

In the case of the Millennials, their skills at using technology may become weaknesses if they rely too much upon data or technical solutions to problems. Over-reliance on social networking could interfere with their ability to form face-to-face connections with real people.

In order to survive in the real world Millennials need to be challenged to rethink some of their perceptions, expectations and preferences. Unlike the

comforting environment of their schools and family, the average workplace probably won't cater much to new Millennial employees' needs and desires. Specifically, Millennials looking to succeed in an exciting new career would benefit from
considering the following advice:

1. Tone Down the Tech
As a Millennial you are most likely a master of technology and possess
strong skills using computers, smart phones, most software and innumerable forms of social media. While these might prove to be strengths
among many employees they become liabilities when Millennial employees, such as yourself, hide behind technology rather than deal with
people face-to-face or voice-to-voice. In the long run interpersonal skills
are far more important for you to develop than technology skills.

2. Replace Virtual Networks with Human Networks
No matter how many friends you may have on Facebook, MySpace,
Twitter, LinkedIn or any of the numerous other social networking sites,
those "contacts" are not highly likely to contribute much to your career
growth. The connections you should be making are with bosses, fellow
employees, customers, suppliers, competitors and other peers. Mentors are another valuable face-to-face relationship to cultivate. "Human
networks" can best be cultivated by talking, meeting and working face-
to-face with people in the real world, rather than online. In the long run
your human network will pay off in tangible benefits. It can also be a lot
more fun to develop.

3. Plan to Succeed by Failing
As a "Trophy Kid" you've been indoctrinated into a cult of "success" and
most likely expect to do well at everything you put your mind to. But
it's a mistake to dismiss the value of failure. There is little to be learned
from success, which is its own reward. But the value of failure runs
much deeper. Through failure you learn what doesn't work and which
mistakes to avoid. Failure better equips you for the future and is actually
the foundation for success. The sooner you make mistakes and fail the
faster you will move along the path to success.

4. Try a Little Humility
Confidence is an invaluable trait that can help foster your success.
While many members of Generation Y are noted for their evident self-
assurance, that quality may not be as useful over the course of your career as humility. You're going to make mistakes and experience failure, as
noted above. However, when you *are* successful you gain much more by
exercising a little humility, rather than demonstrating pride. A humble

---

Millennials and Finding a Mentor

Investor Warren Buffet believes that mentoring, which can be an invaluable career development tool for rising managers, occurs simply because a prospective protégé did something that caught the eye of a potential mentor. As Buffet explained, "Mentoring relationships all just evolve. I never set out to become a mentor. It's amazing how the people that really want to do a terrific job just jump out. There aren't that many. You will be perceived as exceptional and as a worthy person for a superior to spend some extra time with if you just do something extra all the time. It seems elementary, but it's true." 7

---

employee or manager gives credit for the contributions of others. He or she thanks people for their support and focuses upon the benefits to the organization, and not just his or her career. A little humility such as that can take you far in your career!

5. Adopt a Realistic Sense of Ambition

As a Millennial many others see you as self-confident, impatient and ambitious. Some call it a sense of entitlement when young Millennial employees believe they should be promoted after only a short time on the job, or even be hired into a supervisory position directly from school. Once again, your generation -- the "Trophy Kids" -- expect to do well, and there's no reason to believe you won't, given the chance. But at the same time there's no substitute for hard work, paying some dues and earning promotions. You need to understand that success won't be handed to you, so you need a realistic sense of how you will be able to succeed. Having a plan doesn't hurt either!

6. Do Something Extra

As a Millennial your are probably very good at following carefully detailed assignments and doing everything that's expected of you. However, many supervisors complain that their Millennial workers have a hard time going beyond what's expected and anticipating the next task that needs to be done. Unfortunately, your path to career success won't be built upon making just the minimum effort required. Employees who rise to the top of an organization tend to be those who can anticipate what needs to be done and then take the necessary action. No matter how small your contribution may be, you need to take it upon yourself to do something extra every day. That's what will get you the attention and opportunities you need to climb the corporate ladder.

7. Always Be Ten Minutes Early

It may seem petty to base judgments about Millennials' "promote-ability" on whether or not they show up on time. But in the larger world of work punctuality speaks volumes about your character and potential. Being the last employee to stroll though the door at starting time (or after starting time) shows that you may possess a casual disregard for fellow employees who arrived on time (or earlier). Arriving late for meetings wastes everyone's time and interferes with productivity. As a matter of simple respect you would do well to adopt a "10 minutes early" policy at all times. Not only will that boost your productivity, it will also win the respect and gratitude of other employees.

8. Try 'Single-Tasking' From Time to Time

Generation Y is famous for being able to do many things at once. Although they didn't invent the concept, multi-tasking is your generation's claim to fame and you've probably been doing it since childhood. In a busy office environment that skillset may seem to be your advantage for getting things done. But not all tasks can be performed well when you are distracted. When accuracy and detail are critical factors, single-tasking should be the order of the day for you. Doing many things at the same time haphazardly (or even just acceptably) is no substitute for doing one thing really well.

9. Seek Facts Rather than Opinion

Thanks to the Internet we live a world awash with opinions. From social networking, to blogs, news and product-review sites you and your Millennial brethren are flooded daily with comments, reactions, "likes," ratings, rants, tweets, evaluations, editorials, complaints and numerous other forms of opinion. Opinion, in today's society, is ubiquitous throughout all forms of media. Finding the truth is becoming much harder to do. Yet, your career success depends increasingly upon your ability to separate facts from fiction and to distinguish the true from the false. But seeking the truth isn't easy. That will require you to challenge assumptions, ask tough questions, and maintain a healthy skepticism.

10. Recognize the Value of Criticism

For a generation that was virtually raised on positive reinforcement and lavish encouragement, Millennials can be surprisingly sensitive to criticism and negative feedback. All those trophies, awards, and plaques make it tougher for many members of your generation to listen to criticism, despite the value of such feedback. Poorly worded criticism is obviously difficult to absorb and pure insults are unacceptable. But most feedback offers you insights and opportunities to learn and improve."

The Millennial in the Mirror

Whether we like Millennial employees or not, and whether we look forward to the cultural transformations that the Millennial generation most likely will be imposing, we have to admit one thing … we need Millennials in the workplace.

Millennial employees bring energy, hope, enthusiasm and dreams to a workplace that has been long dominated by Baby Boomers, Gen Xers and Matures. Perhaps we did mollycoddle them. Perhaps their expectations of themselves are unrealistically high. And perhaps as a generation we made them what they are. After all, how far can the acorn really fall from the tree? However, like every generation before them they will be somewhat like their parents, somewhat different, and, for at least a period of time, they'll be somewhat ahead of the game.

It's a maxim that everyone had to start somewhere. The Baby Boomers and Gen Xers that preceded the Millennial generation were also the "rookies" on the team at the beginning of their careers and they too had to learn the ropes (often the hard way). But somehow the world survived and sometime in the not-so-distant future the Millennial generation will gradually begin to take charge.

But, if we remain informed and inspired by the potential of this up-and-coming generation then we really have little to fear about the future. The Millennials ultimately will have to assume the mantle of leadership in America and around the globe, a role for which we can only hope they will be prepared. Millennials *are* the future. And that future is… now!

Chapter 8 Notes

1. Malone, N. (2011, October 16). The Kids Are Actually Sort of Alright. Retrieved October 15, 2013, from http://nymag.com/news/features/my-generation-2011-10/

2. Massey, M. (2006, January 1). What You Are Is Where You Were When… Again! With Morris Massey Multimedia DVD – January 1, 2006. Retrieved October 4, 2013, from http://www.amazon.com/What-Where-Again-Morris-Massey/dp/B0035M3I22

3. Nazar, J. (2013, July 23). 20 Things 20-Year-Olds Don't Get. Retrieved April 18, 2014, from http://www.forbes.com/sites/jasonnazar/2013/07/23/20-things-20-year-olds-dont-get/

4, Crouch, A. (2013, December 31). 8 Tips for Millennials to Make 2014 Their Best Year Yet. Retrieved February 12, 2014, from http://www.huffingtonpost.com/ashley-crouch/8-tips-for-millennials-to-make-2014-their-best-year-yet_b_4520606.html

5. Goodman, N. (2012, October 12). James Dyson on Using Failure to Drive Success. Retrieved November 20, 2013, from http://www.entrepreneur.com/blog/224855#ixzz2rdv46KxC

6. Pitino, R., & Crawford, E. (2013). The one-day contract: How to add value to every minute of your life. New York: St. Martin's Press.

7. Guey, V., & Guey, L. (2013, May 8). Warren Buffett Shared Some Great Career Advice For Millennials. Retrieved December 17, 2013, from http://www.businessinsider.com/warren-buffett-becomes-a-mentor-to-young-women-2013-5

8. Lowrey, A. (2013, March 26). Do Millennials Stand a Chance in the Real World? New York Times Magazine, MM12-MM12.